The Fall of the US Dollar A Second Coming of the Non-Aggression Pact

Anthony of Boston

The Fall of the US Dollar
A Second Coming of the Non-Aggression Pact

Table of Contents

Chapter 1: The Fall of the US Dollar

The US dollar has already loss 6% of its value between 2002 and 2018 as a result of the US national debt going from 6 trillion to 23 trillion between that time. If the dollar loses its status as the global reserve currency when Saudi Arabia stops selling oil for US dollars, the dollar would decline far more significantly in value. The US economy maintains a large trade deficit and budget deficit. Back in 2006, the trade deficit amounted to a high of roughly 5% of the GDP, and later in 2020, the budget deficit would account for as high as 15% of the GDP. The presence of these two deficits has caused alarm among economists who believe that the US dollar is headed for a sharp loss of value, one in which the transition between an expansive economic growth and a significant economic slowdown would arise suddenly–a consequence that would lead to a large outflow of capital. Macroeconomists have warned for a number of years that the large US deficits are unmanageable and could negatively impact economic stability not just in the US, but all over the world. And some fear that the rising deficits could hamper the large capital inflows that are used to pay for the ballooning deficits. If the deficit and national debt reach unparalleled levels, and at the same time Saudi Arabia stops selling oil in US dollars, such a sequence of developments could cause more foreign investors to start dumping their treasury bonds and at the same time prevent them from buying new ones. Stakeholders could also ditch their dollar-denominated assets, and seek to invest in other currencies. This outflow of capital could force the Federal Reserve to order the US Bureau of Engraving and Printing to print more money so that the deficit and national debt can be paid and the US can prevent going into default. However, the added printing would lead to widespread inflation and price hikes. Pensions and savings would lose their value, which would affect the elderly and disabled community. The only upside for the US in this currency devaluation scenario is a more competitive export market. But in the meantime, prices in the US would continue to rise as inflation becomes hyperinflation. The dollar then continues to lose value and the US's non-dollar denominated debts become more and more expensive and unmanageable. The US then finds itself on the verge of going into default. Consequently, they try to use up their IMF Special Drawing Rights(SDR) allocation to pay down some of the national debt, but its not enough because the depreciation of the US dollar and it being one of the currencies within the basket of currencies backing the Special Drawing Rights has diminished the SDR's overall value. For this reason, the US has to reach out to the IMF for an IMF loan, but the IMF demands that the US government first cut their spending and reduce their subsidized programs, which leads to

millions of Americans dependent on social services being forced to find another form of income. Crime rates skyrocket. The US tries to reach out to the EU for a loan but Germany refuses because of tensions that arose after the US tried to place an oil embargo on Saudi Arabia after Saudi Arabia chose to sell its oil for Deutchmarks or Euros. Pressure then rises on the Federal Reserve to raise interest rates, as the government is forced by the IMF to pursue austerity measures in order to receive the IMF loan. Unemployment begins to rise as companies start laying off workers and cutting expenses. Those living in subsidized housing are now forced to pay rent, but since jobs are scarce, they cannot find employment and thus become homeless. The US looks to Bitcoin to prop up the value of the US dollar, before trying to liquidate Bitcoin holdings overseas for hard currency, but a new multilateral bloc of nations against US unipolarism impose simultaneous bans on cryptocurrencies, cutting off liquidity. Civil unrest breaks out and communist and ethnocentric factions begin organizing throughout the United States as the wealth gap expands. Lynchings and political assassinations become commonplace. The growing communist movement in the US demands that the Fed loosen monetary policies. Some states give in, other do not. As a consequence, many states along the border that deem themselves more fiscally responsible begin stamping their currency, printing their own currency, and closing their borders and mobilizing state-sponsored militia groups. Articles of secession are filed, but the federal government rejects them and threatens military force against various border states, before deploying federal troops to states threatening secession. The federal government claims the deployment is for the sake of protecting federal property. But some states declare eminent domain and try to seize federal property, and a standoff ensues, and then bloodshed. The US federal government is accused by the international community of committing war crimes, and the condemnation is followed by widespread sanctions. China halts lithium ion battery exports to the United States, compromising US defense capabilities. Russia extends its stoppage of fertilizer exports to the US. Now Europe gets involved. England and France come to the US to help negotiate a ceasefire between seceding states and the federal government. The Russians arrive in Latin America seeking to provide military aid to separatist groups in America via the Mexico/Texas border. Texas becomes the "Ukraine" of the American continent as secessionists seize the opportunity to declare independence. Both Mexico and Russia officially recognize the Texas republic. The war becomes ongoing, but in the end the landscape of North America becomes unrecognizable. The United States has fallen.

The domestic, foreign, and economic policies pursued by the United States in recent years has put the country's prospect of survival in dire straits. And the above scenario is a very real possibility—most noteworthy, the rise of communist sentiments in America, a prospect that has gone on the back-burner, thanks largely in part to America's financial institutions maintaining a long-standing application of expansionary monetary policies and quantitative easing. Now with inflation on the verge of going out of control along with the procrastination by policymakers in raising interest rates to correct it, the US economy has reached a point in which any attempts by policymakers to intervene at a later date when inflation become hyperinflation will come with serious economic repercussions that Americans are not ready to face. This late intervention will create serious financial hardship for a multitude of Americans and will provide an opening for the latent communist movements that have been brewing in the shadows of American civic life in recent years. This threat will ensure that inflation remain a problem in America for years to come because in order to curtail growing widespread political support for the communists, policymakers will find themselves having to give in to demands for expansionary and inflationary monetary policy implementations, which will only further exacerbate inflation. This is the consequence of waiting too late to deal with the issue.

The rise of inflation has reignited debate on whether or not the Federal Reserve should remain. While the Federal Reserve has certainly been instrumental in reducing significantly the prospect of bank runs, they have nevertheless come under intense scrutiny regarding their ability to curtail inflation. The Federal Reserve runs the printing press for dollar bills. They don't print the actual paper currency, but they determine how much is to be printed each year. The actual job of printing paper currency belongs to the Treasury Department Bureau of Engraving and Printing(BEP). (Coins are produced by the U.S. Mint). Basically, the Federal Reserve submits an order to the BEP, who then prints the money and sends it to the Federal Reserve. The Federal Reserve then distributes it to its 28 cash offices, who in turn distribute the money to 8400 banks and credit unions across the country. Those banks and credit unions hold the money as reserves, and the amount they are to lend out is determined by the Federal Reserve Board of Governors, which is comprised of 7 members, all nominated by the President and confirmed by the Senate. The 7 members of the Federal Reserve Board of Governors all serve on the Federal Open Market Committee. All except the Chair and Vice Chair serve 14 year terms. The Chair and Vice Chair only serve 4 year terms. For the 2020 fiscal year, the Federal Reserve ordered 5.2 billion US currency notes valued at 146 billion. So when economic discourse mentions the Fed printing money, this is what they mean. These days, the American money supply is digitally credited or debited to the major banks, and it is not until after the banks loan this money out to the public that the money gets printed. The amount determined to be printed is discussed among the Federal Open Market Committee(FOMC) and its associated economic advisers. The FOMC is a committee within the Federal Reserve and is their monetary policy making body. They have 8 regularly scheduled meetings throughout the year where they discuss monetary policy, interest rates, and economic conditions. The Fed raises interest rates by influencing the Federal Funds rate, which are the reserves held by banks at one of the 12 regional Federal Reserve banks. At the meetings of the FOMC, the Federal Reserve sets a target for the Federal Funds rate, which defines the interest rate at which commercial banks borrow and lend their excess reserves to each other. The Federal Reserve gets banks to raise or lower their interest rates by either increasing the amount required to be held in reserve or reducing the amount required. When the Federal Reserve increases the amount required to be held in reserve, banks become limited in the amount they can lend out. When the Fed decreases the amount required to be held in reserve, the banks can then lend out more. The Federal Reserve can also influence interest rates by changing the interest rate the Federal Reserve bank pays on reserve balances. This sets an upper limit on the fed funds rate since banks will never opt to borrow from another bank at a higher interest rate than what they would get if they simply borrow directly from the Federal Reserve bank. When the economy does not respond to interest rate cuts, the Federal Reserve turns to Quantitative Easing(QE) through its Open Market Operations in order to help stimulate the economy. They began buying up Government Debt and Mortgage backed securities, reducing the supply of these in the market. By purchasing Mortgage backed securities, the Federal Reserve stabilizes the real estate industry, preventing job losses and increasing investor willingness to buy new mortgages. When the Federal Reserve buys US treasury securities, it raises the money supply and increases the volume of bank reserves. Reducing the pace of these QE activities is called tapering. Tapering can slowdown the economy without a corresponding interest rate hike of short term loans.

Prior to the establishment of the Federal Reserve, America's money supply was controlled by the First Bank of the United States, established in 1791 and then later the Second Bank of the United States, established in 1816. The First Bank of the United States was established by Congress at the request of Treasury Secretary Alexander Hamilton and was the largest corporation in the country, but largely opposed by rural Americans who were uncomfortable with such a powerful entity. When the bank's charter expired in 1811 (after 20 years), Congress voted against a new one. In 1816, however, politicians developed renewed fervor for the creation of a central bank, and this is when Congress decided to charter the Second Bank of the United States. But when Andrew Jackson became President in 1828, he vowed to destroy it. He appealed to populist sentiments by criticizing the bank's banker-controlled power, and by 1836, when the bank's charter expired, Congress refused to renew it. Andrew Jackson would manage to pay off all of America's interest bearing debt by selling off government-owned land, but left the country without a uniform national currency. After the Second National Bank expired, the nation's money supply consisted of private bank notes issued by state-charted banks, and were redeemable for gold or silver. Such form of currency system was highly chaotic and by the 1860s, there were 8000 different private bank notes circulating in the US. In some cases, banks would not accept notes issued by banks unknown to them. Ultimately, the rising volume of check transactions led to the creation of the New York Clearinghouse Association in 1853, which allowed banks to exchange checks and settle accounts. These banks also offered demand deposits, which are simply bank deposits that can be withdrawn at any time without advanced notice.

During the American Civil War, the National Banking Act of 1863 was passed. This established nationally chartered banks which issued notes backed by government-owned securities, and also provided the country with a national currency, allowing the government to finance the Union Army during the American Civil War. These paper notes were called greenbacks because of the green print on the back, and were printed in two forms: Demand Notes and United States Notes. In July of 1861, Congress authorized the printing of 50,000,00 in Demand Notes for the purpose of financing the Civil War. These notes could be redeemed for gold or specie; specie is money in the form of coin. The United States Notes, on the other hand, were not backed by anything, but considered equivalent to the Demand Notes. Because of the threat of a severe debt crisis, Congress was urged to pass the "Legal Tender Act" in 1862 which authorized the printing of 150,000,000 in United States Notes. Meanwhile, the Demand Notes were gradually taken out of circulation by mid-1863. The value of the United States Note in relation to gold would fluctuate until after the Civil War when it rose to become on par with gold. When this happened, the United States Notes became convertible into gold. Yet despite the currency stability provided by the National Banking Act of 1863, bank runs and financial panics continued to negatively affect the economy. In 1893, a banking panic triggered a devastating depression in which 575 banks failed or suspended their operations. It was common for banks to suspend operations in order to avoid becoming insolvent by having to liquidate their assets in order to meet the withdrawal demands of depositors. Subsequently, the economy didn't stabilize

until J.P. Morgan intervened.

The Bank Panic of 1907 is what led to the creation of the Federal Reserve System and took place between Oct 14, 1907 – Nov 6, 1907. It was triggered by a stock manipulation scheme intended to force short sellers to cover their positions by buying back their borrowed shares. F Augustus Heinz, a mining magnate who owned stock in United Copper Company believed that short sellers were driving down the price of the stock. Together, he, his brother--broker Otto Heinze, and Wall Street banker Charles W. Morse devised a strategy to force the short sellers to cover their positions and thus create buying pressure that would drive the price of the stock higher. The plan was to aggressively purchase shares of United Copper Company so that the short sellers would have no choice but to buy back their borrowed shares from the Heinzes, who could simply name their price. However, the short sellers were able to find cheaper United Copper Company shares from other sources. This drove the price of the stock down, quickly causing the share price of United Copper Company to collapse. The State Savings bank of Butte, Montana announced its insolvency as they held large stock positions in United Copper Company, which served as collateral against some of their lending. They were also a correspondent bank with the Mercantile National Bank, of which F Augustus Heinze was President. The now tainted reputation of Heinze and his associates as a result of the failed scheme led to a massive bank run in which depositors rushed to withdraw money from Mercantile and other Heinze-associated banks. The panic spread to all financial institutions tied to anyone who was involved in the manipulation scheme. The panic was later brought under control by financier JP Morgan, who put up much of his own money to stabilize the banking system. He also advised other bankers to do the same. The panic underscored the ineffectiveness of the independent Treasury system, which at the time managed the nation's money supply. An investigation of the crisis led to the creation of the Federal Reserve system. During the intervening period, as this bank panic led to growing demands for banking reforms, a consensus for central banking authority and elastic currency grew amongst most Americans. The Aldrich-Vreeland Act was passed in 1908 in response to the panic of 1907 and provided emergency currency issuance during financial crises. It also created the national Monetary Commission to research solutions to the nation's banking problems. The commission developed a banker-controlled plan, but this was largely contested by progressives who wanted a bank under public control, not banker control. However, the election of Woodrow Wilson for President would set the stage for a decentralized central bank, as he would sign the Federal Reserve Act into law in late 1913.

The trade-off that followed the establishment of the Federal

Reserve was the rise of inflation. Before the Federal Reserve System, the US economy was more deflationary. In the 1800s, deflation occurred between 1817 and 1860 & between 1865 and 1900. From 1800 to 1940, the cost of living had risen on average only 0.2% a year. It actually declined on 69 occasions. The average annual inflation between 1790 and 1914 was only 0.4%. In contrast, the average annual inflation between 1914 and 2021 was 3.24%. After 1913, deflation was rare, only occurring between 1930 – 1933 and between 2007-2009. The rise of inflation after 1913 can be attributed to both the elimination of the gold standard and the monetary operations of the Federal Reserve.

From 1929 to 1932, the economy tumbled in what was the beginning of the Great Depression. The stock market crash began on October 24th 1929, Black Thursday, and continued until Tuesday of the next week, October 29th 1929, known as Black Tuesday. The 1920s was marked by economic prosperity, and it was believed that the market would rise forever. In March of 1929, however, the Federal Reserve warned of excessive speculation just before a brief slide. Measures taken to curb speculation could be factored in as catalyst for the crash, since speculation played a large role in the market expansion throughout the 1920s. Banks putting deposits in the stock market was considered as another reason for the crash. The economic downturn from 1930 to 1933 was the first time the US entered a period of deflation after the creation of the Federal Reserve in 1913. It would not encounter deflation again until the 2007-2008 financial crisis.

In 1973 and 1974, the global economy was in a recession, due in large part to a steel crisis, the 1973 oil crisis, and the fall of the Bretton Woods system. More nations were becoming industrialized, and this triggered more competition in the metals industry. In 1973, however, OPEC announced an embargo to all nations supporting Israel during the Yom Kippur war. This, to the detriment of those nations which were heavily dependent on oil. Meanwhile, the rise of dollar printing would become ignited when in 1971, the US pulled out of the Bretton Woods accord where the US dollar was pegged to the price of gold at 35 dollars an ounce, with all other currencies pegged to the dollar.

The Bretton Woods accord was a new global economic order established in Bretton Woods, New Hampshire in July of 1944. Delegates from 44 nations devised an international monetary system known as the Bretton Woods system in order to circumvent barriers that prevented nations from fully cooperating with each other on the international scene. After World War I, the classic gold standard had been abandoned by much of the world, which led to widespread devaluation of national currencies for the sake of gaining trade advantages. Nations were also imposing trade restrictions and protectionist policies, both of which exacerbated the Great Depression. At Bretton Woods, those in attendance formulated an international monetary system that would discourage currency devaluations and at the same time foster economic growth. The primary flow of ideas concerning this new economic system came from John Maynard Keynes, who was an adviser to the British Treasury, and Harry Dexter White, the chief economist at the Treasury Department. Keynes proposed the creation of a large global central bank that would intervene on the global economy when imbalances occurred. This bank would be called the Clearing Union and it would issue a global currency called the "bancor", which would be used to correct international imbalances. Each nation would receive a line of credit to help offset the problems of becoming a net consumer, which is basically the result of a nation importing more goods than it exports. This line of credit was also meant to discourage nations from running a surplus—that is, exporting more goods than it imports—since doing so would require canceling excess bancor to the Clearing Union. White, on the other hand, proposed that the new monetary system maintain a Stabilization Fund that would be funded with a number of national currencies and gold worth 5 million which would limit the amount of reserve credit. The plan that was chosen followed along the lines of White's proposal. However, Keynes concern about nations running surpluses was accounted for with the idea that a clause can be added which would permit the fund to ration the currency of the nation that was running the surplus. It was also decided that the total resources of the fund would be increased from 5 million to 8.5 million. The 730 delegates at Bretton Woods agreed to establish 2 institutions. The first was "The International Monetary Fund"(IMF), which would watch over exchange rates and lend reserve currencies to nations running balance of payment deficits as a result of importing more than they are exporting. The second was the World Bank Group, which would be responsible for giving financial assistance both to nations rebuilding after World War II, and to emerging nations that were looking to develop economically. The IMF was formalized in 1945, as member countries agreed to keep their currencies pegged to the dollar, while the dollar would be pegged to gold at 35 dollars an ounce. By 1958, this system would become fully functional. In 1969, the IMF created its own reserve asset called the Special Drawing Rights (SDR), which is backed by a basket of currencies that figure prominently in international transactions. The IMF's financial arrangements with member countries are denominated in SDR, and each member country is allocated a portion of SDR based on economic and currency factors(nations with stronger economies tend to have higher SDR quotas and allocation). By exchanging the SDR with other member nations for hard currencies, nations are better able pay off their debts. The IMF also issues hard currency loans to nations experiencing financial difficulty.

After the IMF was initially created, the United States was to be responsible for keeping the price of gold fixed and adjusting the supply of dollars to help foster confidence in gold convertibility. The Bretton Woods system held steady until US balance-of-payments deficits created an imbalance in which foreign- held dollars would exceed the amount of US gold stock.

The dollar had been freely exchangeable into gold, but when the US pulled out of the Bretton Woods accord in 1971, convertibility into gold was no longer tenable since America's stores of gold had depleted over time. Thus the dollar became a fiat currency backed by nothing, that is, until the Petrodollar Agreement was established by President Richard Nixon and Secretary of State Henry Kissinger in 1973, as the collapse of the gold standard triggered a worldwide bear market. The basic gist of the agreement was that the US would agree to defend Saudi Arabia militarily in return for all oil becoming denominated in US dollars. Another option of this arrangement would be the purchase of US Treasury Securities with the extra profits from oil sales. Shortly thereafter, an accordance was established in 1975, as Saudi Arabia and all OPEC nations would agree to sell their oil for US dollars and also hold their oil proceeds in US Treasury securities. The US would in exchange agree to provide military support and security. The result was that the US dollar became the world's reserve currency since much of the world's energy exchange had be transacted with US dollars. This exponentially increased global demand for US dollars since all foreign governments that relied on oil imports from the middle east had to hold US dollars in order to purchase it. Essentially the US dollar had simply transitioned from the gold standard to the oil standard. And this increased demand for US dollars gave the US more leg room to print higher amounts of money before dangerous levels of inflation could ever set in. The main points of the agreement: The Saudis would sell their oil in US dollars only and invest the surplus profits in US Treasury securities, while the US would agree to assure Saudi Arabia's security with military support.

The standard outlook of intervention is that when inflation is high, the Federal Reserve can normally raise interest rates to slow down the economy. When inflation is low, the Federal Reserve can typically lower rates to speed up the economy. An example of this being applied in real time is when Paul Volcker, the twelfth Chairman of the Board of Governors of the Federal Reserve System, raised interest rates significantly in 1980 in order to bring the down the Great Inflation that occurred throughout the decade of the 1970s.

It is likely that the Great Inflation had come about both as a result of the collapse of Bretton Woods system and as a result of the PetroDollar agreement established in 1973, allowing the US to print more cash due to the higher global demand for US dollars but without any real way to account for the monetary aggregates that are responsible for the financial stability of a nation's monetary system. Money circulation in relation to money held in reserve was hard to keep track of throughout much of the 1970s, but Paul Volker insisted that the FOMC focus on strategies to deal with the growth of monetary aggregates in order to help bring down inflation. Volker would thus raise interest rates to 20% in March of 1980, before lowering it in June. As inflation subsequently rose again, Volcker hiked interest rates back to 20% in December of 1980 and left it above 16% until of May of 1981. Known as the Volcker Shock, this strategy worked and ended the Great Inflation. While this is a simple methodology, it does not eliminate every cause for inflation. While the Federal Reserve can increase or decrease the money supply by raising or lowering the reserve requirements for banks, they still have no control over the price setting by producers of goods and services. Those who sell goods and services can raise prices in response to money tightening implementations and in such a manner that would force policy makers to increase the money supply, further driving inflation. After the 2008 financial crisis, in which the Federal Reserve pumped billions of dollars into investment firms that were on the verge of collapse, the notion of economics took on a considerable change, where money supply became defined in terms of both the amount of it in circulation and the amount of it that could be printed. This is a revolting prospect because now dealers may be less perturbed by fiscal policies aimed at tightening the money supply and reducing inflation. This in itself conjures a reality in which inflation becomes hyperinflation and reaches a point where it will not respond to monetary policy implementations, seeing that in light of the PetroDollar agreement of 1973, producers would insist that the US Treasury Department print more money to keep up with the price of goods. This level of hyperinflation could only be resolved by an overhaul of the current system. Re-institution of the gold standard thus becomes the only solution to curbing inflation. Unless, the Federal Reserve can prove to the economy that simply printing more money is not feasible, even with a backdrop of continuous global demand. This would require another 2008-like financial crisis scenario where firms would be allowed to collapse, as opposed to receiving large sums of bailout funds. The result is the dollar becomes perceived to have more value and as a consequence, inflation comes under control.

In 2008, the stock market experienced one of its worst years, dropping 33%. The Housing bubble and debt bubble were considered major triggers for the 2008 crash. During the housing bubble, investment firms were packaging mortgage loans into securities(Mortgage-backed securities- MBS), and then selling them off to investors, allowing the firm to keep them off their financial statements. Rating agencies rated the MBS, which served as a benchmark for potential buyers. The investors then started using credit default swaps, in which an insurance company would guarantee to cover the any potential losses from the MBS in exchange for a premium. This proved profitable for many investors and insurance companies. However, when investment firms started having trouble finding buyers for their MBS products, along with rating agencies downgrading them as the credit crisis worsened, investment firms were left having to hold large positions in MBS. This is what happened to Bear Sterns in April of 2008 and then Lehman brothers in September of 2008, as both had to declare bankruptcy. AIG, the main underwriter of credit default swaps was bailed out by the Federal Reserve, since the company was designated as Too Big To Fail. AIG provided protections worth half a trillion dollars, 300 billion to banks in the US and Europe. Failure of AIG would have had global implications.

After the Fed bailed out US banks by pumping trillions of dollars into the financial sector after the 2008 financial crisis, inflation did not spike, and this is indicative of how the petrodollar agreement in 1973 provided the US more leg room to provide higher monetary emissions without triggering a correlated risk of high inflation. And in retrospect, the United States lived up to their 1973 petrodollar agreement with OPEC, when in 1989, tension arose between Iraq and Kuwait. Both of these nations are original OPEC member countries, but Iraq accused Kuwait of producing more oil than which was required by the OPEC quota at the time, causing oil prices to drop, which in turn was hurting Iraq's economy and their ability to pay off debts accrued during the Iran-Iraq war from 1980-1988. Iraqi President Saddam Hussein had also accused Kuwait of slant drilling into Iraq's Rumalia oil field, which compelled Saddam to declare war and embark upon an invasion of the country. Iraq's conquest of Kuwait led to the 1991 Gulf War in which a coalition led by the United States intervened and repelled the Iraqi forces from Kuwait, and from further advancing into Saudi Arabia, which was the main concern for the US since Saudi Arabia exports 15% of the world's crude oil reserves—the highest of any nation. There was fear that after Iraq's occupation of Kuwait, Saddam would target Saudi Arabia's oil fields. This defense of Saudi Arabia was main point of the 1973 PetroDollar agreement—Saudi Arabia sell oil for USD and in return the US protect them militarily. However, after the year 2000, a number of OPEC nations decided to stop selling their oil for US dollars. Iraq switched to selling their oil for Euros in the early

2000s. Shortly thereafter, the US invaded Iraq in 2003 without pretext. In 2011, Libya threatened to sell their oil for gold, before Qaddafi, Libya's President at that time, would be ousted and killed via a US-backed coup. In 2012, Iran stopped trading their oil for US dollars, and in 2018, Venezuela followed suit and also decided to stop selling their oil for US dollars. Both nations were slapped with devastating sanctions that ultimately crippled their economies. Saudi Arabia is now the last line of defense for US dollar hegemony and the economic expansion that followed the elimination of the gold standard. But in recent years, the United States has been enveloped within a long-standing disastrous foreign policy approach which had no qualms about giving assurances to militant forces or separatist movements in foreign countries, before abandoning them to the mercy of defeat, which oftentimes devastated the entire country. Such was the case in Vietnam, Syria, and Libya. And now NATO expansion eastward at the behest of the US for the sake of provoking Russia, along with the US's unkept assurances to Ukraine amid a massive Russian invasion of the country has given way to a growing lack of trust in US foreign policy. This will eventually come to a head with regards to US/Saudi relations, which is a critical alliance with systemic implications for the US.

As of 2021, relations between Saudi Arabia and the United States have become strained. Washington D.C. has opted to take a hardline stance against the Saudi Crown Prince and threatened to prosecute him over the killing of Jamal Khashoggi, a Saudi-American journalist who was threatening to reveal damning information about Saudi Arabia's war crimes in Yemen. The US President had also vowed to cut US involvement in Yemen, and at the same time continue to ignore the Yemen issue in nuclear talks with Iran. Yemen is a central issue for Saudi Arabia's security due to the fact that the Iran-backed Houthi militant group has used drones supplied to them by Iran to attack Saudi oil facilities. The US's backstep on these issues could lead to Saudi Arabia cutting ties with the US, and refusing to sell their oil for US dollars. If this is the beginning of a strong rift between the US and Saudi Arabia, it will have an enormous negative impact on the US economy. This is also something that could send gold through the roof. Saudi Arabia has so much clout that it was once classified how Saudi Arabia was abusing their position with the US, helping Saudis accused of crimes in the US evade the US Judicial process by extraditing them back to Saudi Arabia. These crimes included manslaughter, child pornography, and rape. Many don't realize that if Saudi doesn't sell their oil for US dollars, there would be no global demand for US dollars, and hence there would be no way the US treasury could continue to print the infinite amounts of currency they are currently printing. This current discord is a direct result of Washington D.C.'s

combative foreign policy stance since the 2020 US presidential election. The US-Saudi alliance is a critical alliance and the US may need to hope that the Saudis are not planning to look elsewhere for military assurances. Especially with Germany now both re-militarizing in response to the Russian invasion of Ukraine, and also seeking alternative sources of oil... now that Germany's dependence on oil from Russia may be unsustainable as Russia becomes isolated from the international community. With Germany's economic situation at stake, they may look to compete with the US for mid-east influence by using diplomatic backchannels to set up oil deals that could be favorable for the euro and the German economy, and of which would undercut US interests and their economic security. Now that the increased production of arms and innovation could provide Germany with tremendous bargaining power, Saudi Arabia may be tempted to seek out more assertive military assurances from other nations besides the US. As Germany becomes further alienated from Russia diplomatically, it may correspond to a much easier decision on their part to agree to defend Saudi Arabia militarily, and that would include getting involved in the Yemen Crisis. Russia in recent years has tried to expand their influence in the middle east, but their ties to an allied consortium of Shiite nations like Iran and Syria made it impossible for Russia to provide Saudi Arabia with the security guarantees that it needs, if such was in fact on their agenda. The most Russia could offer in their attempt to branch out diplomatically from this consortium was allowing Israel to have unfettered access to Syrian airspace, so that Israel could conduct airstrikes on Iran bases in Syria, bases which are used to channel arms and other supplies to Iranian proxies in Yemen, Lebanon, and the Gaza Strip. These diplomatic limitations for Russia leaves Germany as the next best option for Saudi Arabia's security.

Chapter 2: The Rise of Germany's Currency

Saudi Arabia and Germany have maintained a steady diplomatic relationship, further encouraged by the way German officials would classify Saudi Arabia as an "anchor of stability. This is largely derived from the way Saudi Arabia conducted itself during the Arab Spring which occurred in 2011 and affected much of the middle east region. The Arab spring was a string of domestic unrest taking place throughout the Arab world. It started in Tunisia and spread to Libya, Egypt, Yemen, Syria, and Bahrain. Saudi Arabia, however, remained for the most part unaffected. The relations between Saudi Arabia and Germany are sustained on a mutual desire by both nations to foster cooperation on dealing with issues like terrorism and instability. Both Germany and Saudi Arabia share intelligence and each country's domestic security benefits as a result. Saudi Arabia has been instrumental in providing tips to the German government about extremist networks, and has aided Germany's ability to uncover terrorist plots. In terms of economics, Germany is a main supplier of arms and other machinery to Saudi Arabia. A number of German companies have also opened businesses in Saudi Arabia, which increased the trade volume between the two nations.

On the negative side, as a result of growing right wing extremism in Germany, Saudi Arabia is oftentimes perceived negatively as a nation that is defined by misogyny, discrimination, and a poor human rights record. Many point to the Islamic fundamentalist sects in Saudi Arabia as the essence of the country, and a number of German citizens are critical of Germany's export of arms to the country. Much of Saudi Arabia's image in Germany is backed by a great deal of ignorance and lack of scholarship on the country, as only a handful of Germany's academic researchers and writers have been permitted to visit there. There is essentially no thorough analysis of the Saudi civil society which can be presented to Germans for a more accurate picture, and German media coverage of what happens in Saudi Arabia has been limited. Much of this restrained approach is bound to the fact that the German/Saudi relations are pragmatically trade and security related, with each preferring to stay out of the political affairs of the other. Since 2011 when Saudi Arabia showed itself stable amid regional geopolitical unrest, the Germans took a heightened interest in Saudi Arabia politically. This was clear when in 2018 after the murder of Jamal Khashoggi, a Saudi-American journalist, Germany imposed an arms embargo on Saudi Arabia.

Saudi Arabia has proven itself to be the strongest and most stable Mideast nation, and this has led to a growing German presence in Saudi affairs. High ranking officials in both nations embarked upon diplomatic visits to the other's country, and Germany was delighted when King Salman was inaugurated in 2015, with his youngest son,

Muhammad Bin Salman(MBS), appointed to Minister of Defense. However when Bin Salman was appointed Crown Prince in 2017, after King Salman deposed bin Nayef, he became the heir to the throne. This was controversial, and the move was foreseen in a memo published by German Federal Intelligence Service, indicating Germany's heightened interest in Saudi politics.

MBS's move to modernize Saudi Arabia with the "Vision 2030" plan, which allowed women to drive and theaters to open, was covered extensively by the German media and presented Saudi Arabia in a positive light. However, the scrutiny of Saudi Affairs by the German Federal Intelligence service was seen as aggressive. Another report about MBS policy was leaked in December of 2015, and in the report, German intelligence service wrote about how MBS's foreign policy was reckless and militaristic. This gave off the impression that Saudi Arabia is willing to assert its itself politically and militaristically without regard for international ramifications. Many German citizens became concerned in 2015 about the human rights implications surrounding the Saudi-led military campaign in Yemen. Another controversy was Saudi Arabia's role in helping initiate the blockade against Qatar in 2017.

When it comes to Saudi Arabia's domestic affairs, Germany had become concerned about the harsh measures that Saudi officials imposed on various critics of the Saudi government. These critics ranged from political, media, and economic figures. A number of human rights activists that Saudi officials felt threatened by were detained. These occurrences have led to more discussion in Germany about the need to assert more pressure on Saudi Arabia to scale down its harsh policies. Ultimately, the main concern of German citizens is Germany's arms exports to Saudi Arabia. After Saudi journalist Jamal Khashoggi was murdered and dismembered in the Saudi consulate in Turkey, Germany declared that it would cease arms exports to Saudi Arabia. Germany also requested that a throughout investigation into the murder be initiated. In the mean time, due to the Khashoggi incident, Germany postponed German Foreign Minister Heiko Maas's diplomatic trip to Saudi Arabia.

When it comes the way Saudi Arabia assesses their relations with Germany, they consider Germany a reliable partner and don't hold any long-standing grievances against Germany. Germany has no colonial history in the Saudi region, which puts relations between Germany and Saudi Arabia on a good starting point. However, Germany's involvement in the Joint Comprehensive Plan of Action (JCPoA) with Iran has brought into question the nature of Germany's desire to establish trust with the Saudi government. The Saudis and the Iranians have been locked in a proxy war in Yemen. Thus the Saudis are more inclined and in favor of Germany showing more solidarity with the Saudi government by distancing itself from Iran. Germany's involvement with Iran has drawn some suspicion from Saudi officials, who once accused German Foreign Minister Sigmar Gabriel of being an Iranian agent. This suspicion of Germany among the Saudis became heightened after German Foreign Minister Sigmar Gabriel blamed Saudi Arabian influence for the resignation of Lebanon's Prime Minister Saad Hariri. He referred to the situation using the term "adventurism" to describe the Saudi's influence over the affair. Appalled at the rhetoric, Saudi Arabia pulled its own ambassador HRH Prince Khalid bin Bandar Al Saud out of Germany. This led to a fallback in Saudi/Germany bilateral economic relations. Saudi Arabia ordered Saudi ministries to stop conducting business with German companies, and also restricted German politicians from entering the country. Soon enough, however, this protest was ended and Saudi officials looked forward to restoring normalized relations with Germany.

Other areas of German standards that Saudi officials have been critical of is what they see as Germany's risk aversion. And more disappointing to Saudi business officials is the apprehension of Germany to invest more in Saudi Arabia. Saudi Arabia has tried to persuade Germany to invest more, asserting that in order for "Vision 2030" to become a reality, more investment is needed. There is a bit of a mix-up in terms of what each country is expecting from the other. Germany wants to establish relations based more on trade than direct investment into Saudi Arabia, whereas Saudi Arabia is expecting Germany to offer more direct investment into Saudi Arabia. Saudi Arabia has high expectations for the partnership.

The diplomatic crisis that unfolded between Germany and Saudi Arabia over the Khashoggi incident, the Lebanon Prime Minister affair, and Germany's involvement with Iran has led to a decrease in bilateral trade volume. The German export volume to Saudi Arabia decreased 13% in the first quarter of 2008. This indicates that Saudi's image of Germany as a trustworthy trading partner has diminished. This also explains why Saudi Arabia has spent a great deal of time reaching out eastward to South Korea and China, even considering selling their oil to the Chinese in 2022 for Chinese Yuan instead of US dollars.

Overall, Germany holds no significant influence over Saudi affairs compared to other nations like France, the UK, and the US. In Germany, Saudi Arabia is still perceived to be somewhat outside the bounds of German cultural and progressive tastes despite the fact that MBS has been pushing for cultural advances in Saudi Arabia, such as allowing women to drive and permitting women to travel alone in public without being accompanied by a male guardian, spouse, or sponsor. Since 2018, there have been small steps by Germany and Saudi Arabia in the direction of improving bilateral relations. Saudi Arabia considers Germany's innovative sector as something that could foster potential for a multitude of Saudi industries like healthcare, pharmaceutical, and education system. And this could payoff immensely for German investors. One of the main purposes of "Vision 2030" is not just the aim to modernize Saudi Arabia, but also to cultivate an environment that will attract foreign investment. Much of the Arab world as been embroiled in geopolitical issues for some time, but Saudi Arabia has been the pillar of stability and Saudi Arabia has presented a progressive plan alongside this aspect of stability that should compel foreign investment. Policies have already been enacted in Saudi Arabia that will ultimately set women on the path to becoming a major catalyst for economic and social change.

From the vantage point of Saudi Arabia, this "new Saudi Arabia" that is in the works would be unprecedented in Mideast affairs and could have a trickle down effect to much of the Arab world. Such a prospect should further open the door to a more complete engagement on the part of Germany. The changes are already underway in Saudi Arabia and many young upstarts in Saudi Arabia have expressed a desire to establish stronger ties with colleagues in Germany who are also in the start-up sectors. Many in the start-up hub in Saudi Arabia have expressed a desire to work in the fields of renewable energy, and artificial intelligence which makes for great partnership opportunities.

Saudi Arabia has great respect for Germany's achievements in culture and the arts, and respects Germany's contributions in the fields of literature, music, and opera. The German embassy in Riyadh has already organized cultural festivities like hip hop concerts, and looks forward to pursuing further opportunities for cooperation in this area, as well as opportunities for Saudi performers to present their artistic qualities in Germany which could perhaps provide insight to Germans about Saudi civic life. One of the biggest hurdles to establishing a cultural correspondence is rising Islamophobia which could upend German sentiment about German/Saudi relations. However, Saudi Arabia's efforts to improve the outlook of Islamic nations through modernization could certainly overcome the detriments of Islamophobia.

One of the biggest contributions the Germans can offer in its economic relations with Saudi Arabia is by expanding exchange programs. Giving Saudi students access to German academic institutions will allow more Saudis to gain more understanding German culture.

Overall, many of the challenges that could impede the development of greater bilateral relations between Saudi Arabia and Germany are still possible to defeat. The ability to overcome the diplomatic fallback originating from ongoing discourse about issues of Saudi Arabia's human rights record, Germany's growing far right Islamophobia, the Saudi-led military operations in Yemen, and the murder of Jamal Khashoggi will be dependent on how Germany takes to Saudi Arabia's "Vision 2030" initiative.

The crisis in Yemen has turned out to be a major humanitarian crisis, and Saudi involvement has served as a roadblock to further improvements in Saudi/German relations. The Yemen civil war started in the aftermath of the Arab Spring in 2011 which led to the ousting of Yemen President Ali Abdullah Saleh, who had ruled Yemen for 33 years. The anti-government movement consisted of numerous factions, all of whom insisted on Saleh's departure. In 2012, Abdrabbuh Mansur Hadi was elected to President of Yemen, replacing Saleh. But Hadi would be unsuccessful in uniting the various anti-government factions, and he also refused to appoint any Houthis to his cabinet. The Houthis had been fighting an insurgency in northern Yemen since 2004, when the government at that time accused the Houthis of trying to overthrow the administration. The Houthis denied this and had since considered their insurgency a defensive operation against attacks on their community by the north Yemen government. The insurgency was sparked when the Houthi leader Hussein al-Houthi was killed by Yemen government forces in 2004. In the ensuing years, the Houthis would launch attacks against Yemen government forces throughout the northern region and fighting would then shift near the Saudi border. In 2009, the Houthis accused Saudi Arabia of allowing the Yemen military to use their bases to launch attacks on Houthi positions. Subsequently, Houthi militants began a series of attacks on Saudi border guards, which led to a Saudi military response. The Saudis subsequently launched airstrikes in northern Yemen. In 2011, during the Arab Spring, the Houthis pledged their support to the anti-government movements throughout Yemen, before taking over the Sadaa Governorate in northern Yemen. After Hadi came to power in Yemen, his administration was trying to secure a loan from the IMF, which required Hadi to implement austerity measures such as removing subsidies on fuel, which would consequently cause the price of fuel to rise significantly. This move was contested by the Houthis, who would storm the capital, Sanaa, and demand that Hadi draft a new constitution and form a unity government. When the Hadi administration could not present a favorable draft in line with Houthi demands, the Houthis attempted to seize control of the Hadi residential palace, which led to Hadi and his administrative officials resigning in early 2015. Houthi incursion into Sanaa met with little to no resistance from the Yemen army, which allowed the Houthis to establish an interim government. But this new government was not recognized by many of the political entities in Yemen. Shortly thereafter in 2015, Saudi Arabia intervened, leading a coalition of Gulf states who would begin launching airstrikes in Yemen with the intent to restore the Hadi administration. They also initiated a naval blockage against the Houthis. In 2016, the Houthis attempted to restore the Saleh administration that they previously protested against during the

Arab Spring in 2011. The Houthis tried to establish a political council with Saleh, but Saleh would cut ties with the Houthis soon after and encourage his followers to take up arms against them. However, Saleh would be killed a short while later, and his forces would be defeated by the Houthis in 2017. Meanwhile, the Saudi government accused Iran of aiding the Houthi fighters—a fact that had become evident as a number of Iranian weapons had been intercepted in the Gulf of Aden. Houthi fighters in recent years have launched successful drone attacks on Saudi oil facilities. Throughout the conflict, the US has been conducting airstrikes concurrently with the Saudis, but mainly targeting Al Qaeda operatives in the region. These airstrikes, the blockade, water and food shortages has created a humanitarian catastrophe in Yemen with a death toll in the range of 300,000. The US has been conducting airstrikes in Yemen since 2002, and the number of civilians killed during those airstrikes are unknown. Since 2021, the US has stated their intention to withdraw support for the Saudi led intervention in Yemen. However, things took a positive turn in April of 2022 when exiled Yemen President Hadi transferred his presidential powers to a new political council that would negotiate a ceasefire with the Houthis. The truce will allow fuel to be shipped into Yemen. Saudi Arabia has also pledged 3 billion to support the Yemen economy, and also help facilitate negotiations for the Hadi government to include a wider array of political groups. These developments as of April 2022 would decrease Saudi Arabia's urgency for western military support and security assurances, and thus make it unlikely that they would in the near future scout this type of support from nations other than the US. But should the conflict in Yemen re-escalate and the Houthis resume attacks on Saudi and UAE territory, Saudi Arabia could move quickly to find another security partner if the US remains intent on withdrawing military support for Saudi Arabia against the Houthi militants. In that case one can predict that Saudi Arabia will end the petrodollar agreement which involves Saudi Arabia selling their oil for US dollars in exchange for military support from the US. The Saudis will simply offer this type of deal to a nation that could uphold their end of the agreement. Such would result in the immediate collapse of the US dollar, and exponential rise of the currency of which ever nation Saudi chooses to establish this type of agreement with. Still and all, the deescalation in Yemen as of April 2022 opens the door for Germany to further engage Saudi Arabia diplomatically since Germany's negative public outlook of the Saudi intervention in the Yemen crisis would subside as Yemen stabilizes. In this case, there would be less political fallback in terms of how Germany's relations with Saudi Arabia is perceived within Germany. Yemen stabilization allows the Saudi government to present itself as the beacon of hope for the Middle East, which will translate to a more favorable impression internationally, which thus gives German investors more confidence to invest in Saudi Arabia. A growing relationship both politically and economically could make Germany a possible candidate for ensuring Saudi security, and if Saudi Arabia is taking a more persistent approach in resolving geopolitical issue diplomatically, such could make it easier for Germany to pledge military support for the Saudi Kingdom, seeing that German military support will be backing a nation that will be making every effort to reduce the need for their intervention, while at the same time allowing Germany to reap considerable benefits as Saudi Arabia helps foster global demand for the German currency by selling their oil for either Deutschmarks or Euros. The efforts of MBS certainly argues in favor of such a framework. But of course in order for Saudi Arabia to part ways with the United States diplomatically, they would have to foresee security issues on the horizon and presume that the US will not intervene on their behalf. Such a calculation would lead to Saudi Arabia looking elsewhere in order to have security measures in place ahead of time.

Because of this possibility, the Federal Reserve must prepare in advance a contingency plan in the likely event of US dollar collapse. Because as of now in 2022, there are 4 major factors that support the idea of such a scenario arising in the near future. 1. German military buildup and isolation from Russia and their need to secure energy imports and deals from the middle east to make up for the economic fall back. 2. Reckless rhetoric towards Saudi officials by the current 2022 US administration 3. The Federal Reserve's slow response to rising inflation. 4. The world's slow transition to alternative sources of energy.

Chapter 3: Rise of the Russian Ruble

Some argue that the US will soon no longer rely on oil imports from foreign countries, and thus it won't matter if US relations with top oil exporting mideast nations deteriorate. While the United States has been experiencing a shale oil boom in recent years, it is not close to being energy independent. Back in 2006, US President George W Bush told Americans during his State of the Union address that "America is addicted to oil." He declared that America should reduce its reliance in mideast oil and reduce the amount of oil it imports from the middle east. It had been long asserted that US reliance on mideast oil stifles America's foreign policy goals. However, within the last decade, the United States discovered an economically viable way to extract oil from shale rock formations underground, which led to the shale boom that would enable the US to become a net oil exporter in 2019. The drilling technique used to extract oil from shale rocks is called hydraulic fracking, and it involves targeting rock formations underground by injecting mixtures of water, sand and other chemicals at high speeds. Because shale is a finite resource and shale wells normally decline much sooner than conventional wells, US production of oil should not be seen as something that will eliminate America's dependence on foreign oil. Not to mention, it takes 6 months to a year in order to boost shale production. Another constraining factor is the limited amount of equipment, workers, and pipeline infrastructure. And because oil is a global market, any changes in oil production overseas will affect oil prices at home, which could affect profit margins for shale oil companies.

Another argument that is used to convey confidence that the US no longer needs to rely on foreign oil or foreign oil deals is one that points out US efforts in recent years to combat climate change. In order to reduce reliance on oil, the west has been looking to solar and wind energy, which would certainly reduce the world's reliance on petroleum products as far as electricity generation is concerned. Transportation, however, accounts for 71% of US petroleum consumption, and for this reason, the US is still a ways away from long distance electric vehicles or vehicles that could run on 100% bio-fuels. And because of this, one can not argue with certainty that a global shift away from the reliance on oil is underway. At the moment, there are a few vehicles that can run on 10% ethanol 90% gasoline, or 20% bio-diesel 80% petroleum diesel. The use of biomass/bio-diesel/bio-fuels for transportation is still being studied and some researchers are concerned about how it could disrupt food distribution. Russia is certainly a case study; how can grain/wheat be converted into ethanol when the west is facing grain shortages because of the war in Ukraine? And what about how bio- diesel will affect animal life, seeing that much of it is extracted from animal fats. Sure, one can advise that it only be extracted from dead animals, but that will likely not be the case everywhere. Profiteers will have no problem resorting to killing more and more animals just for the sake of attaining greater access to the bio-diesel market. Combine that with the fact that most humans are still carnivores. This literally gives way to a greater demand for dead animals, a prospect that animal rights groups will protest en masse.

In both cases of bio-diesel and ethanol fuels, we have a situation where its production is cutting into food availability. Combine that with the fact that humans still have an affinity for both starting wars and instigating them. So alot of other factors which are still embedded into human society has to change before the world could ever consider a full transition to alternative sources of fuel.

Due to Russia's invasion of Ukraine in February of 2022, worldwide sanctions have been imposed on Russia. These have caused inflation in Russia to rise to nearly 10%, and many analyst are forecasting it will surpass 20% by the end of March 2022 as the Russian currency, the ruble, continues to collapse. Russia relies on imported goods such as cars, household appliances, televisions and smartphones, but multiple sanctions levied by the west against Russia has effectuated massive price increases among those products. The price of new cars rose 15%. Russia is also worried about how a reliance on imports for its agricultural industry, such as potato seeds will affect the economic situation. In response to the rising inflation and as a measure to stabilize prices, Russia's Central Bank has raised interest rates to 20%. According to the BBC, the sanctions applied against Russia for invading Ukraine in 2022 are as follows: The United States banned its oil and gas imports from Russia. The UK said they would gradually phase out their Russian oil imports by 2030. And Germany and the EU pledged to reduce their reliance on Russian oil by seeking alternative sources of energy before 2030. The west has also frozen Russia's foreign holdings of dollars and euros, and restricted banks from doing business with Russia's central bank. Some of Russia's banks are being restricted from the SWIFT banking system, which will prevent them from conducting international transactions. This would also delay any accounts receivable owed to Russia for its oil and gas exports. The UK has frozen the assets of all Russian banks, and restricted their access to the UK financial system. The result is that Russia would not be able to raise funds or borrow money within the UK. A number of goods have been restricted from being sent to Russia, while the UK, US, EU, and Canada have banned Russian airlines from its airspace. Assets belonging to Russian president Vladimir Putin has been frozen as well. Russia in response has banned much of their exports to the west, exports which consist of various products, such as telecoms, medical, vehicle, agricultural, electrical equipment and timber. Russia has also stopped making interest payments to foreign investors holding Russian government bonds, and they also squeezed the liquidity of stocks and bonds held by foreign investors. In light of these developments, one can see how the sanctions will have a detrimental impact on western Europe. Not only in terms of acquiring adequate energy supplies, which might no longer be provided by Russia, but also in terms of food production. Russia and Ukraine account for a third of the world's wheat/grain and barley exports, but now with these sanctions levied upon Russia by the west, along with Russia retaliating by stopping its wheat/grain and fertilizer exports, much of the world that is dependent on such food supplies will have to face the prospect of significant food shortages, and at the same time deal with the impact of how fertilizer shortages will disrupt the very sensitive farming protocols, which could keep crop yields very low. Places like Egypt, Tunisia, and Lebanon are dependent on grain/wheat imported from Russia. Everything considered, Ukraine and Russia are basically world powers in the global food supply industry.

These sanctions against Russia present a catch 22. In one sense, Russia is cut off from the financial sector in the west, but at the same time, they will be able to accrue a surplus inventory from oil and grain production. This leaves the likelihood that Russia will become a major player in ethanol production, as many industries around the world are seeking to transition from 100% petroleum to using a mix of petroleum and biofuels, before eventually going 100% biofuel. With wheat shortages in the west and the middle east, Russia would be able to become the major player in ethanol production since ethanol is produced from wheat and corn, which would be in surplus amounts in Russia as a result of halting their export. This prospect could coincide with a spectacular ruble recovery, should Russia decide to sell ethanol in exchange for rubles and at the same time undercut US corn production by refusing to export nitrogen fertilizer. This would in effect stifle US ethanol production because without adequate fertilizer, the west would not have the surplus corn to produce greater amounts of ethanol. In this scenario, much of the corn would have to be designated for human consumption. As a result of the competition being eroded in the ethanol market, the rising ruble would not undermine the competitive viability of Russia's export of ethanol fuels, should those fuels be sold for rubles. The extra wheat and corn could also be used as a bargaining chip in places like the middle east and Africa, whom will insist on resuming grain imports from Russia. In this manner, Russia could seek out ospolitik-type agreements in which Russia would attempt to normalize relations with other nations by being granted some media influence in exchange for grain shipments or fertilizer. This would be for the sake of controlling how Russia is viewed as a nation within other countries. This would also give Russia more influence in the middle east in terms of being able to mediate peace between warring nations, despite Russia belonging to a consortium of Shiite nations like Syria, and Iran.

A growing dependency on Russia's production of oil, gas, and ethanol blends would bring the west back into Russia's sphere of influence, should urgency about carbon emissions continue to grow worldwide. This would also coincide with a greater global demand for rubles, which would allow Russia to stimulate their economy by safely increasing the amount of rubles circulating within their financial system.

China's financial ties and trading relationship with the United States since 1979, when China joined the World Trade Organization, has been characterized by unfair trading practices in which China would impose much higher tariffs on US goods coming into China than those imposed by the US on Chinese goods coming into the US. Prior to 2018, China's tariffs on US goods were roughly 8%, while US tariffs on Chinese goods were 3%. Many trade analysts felt this arrangement to be unfair. An ensuing trade war between China and the US led to both countries imposing tariffs on the others' exports at around 19-20% circa 2021.

China, throughout its economic relationship with the US, also maintained an approach of orchestrating businesses partnerships with American investors in which the majority of the company would be owned by the Chinese. It was through these ventures that Chinese investors would insist on the transfer of US intellectual property, which ultimately allowed China to replicate what the US produced and thus go from being a trading partner to a direct competitor in that particular market. This undermined the possibility of the joint venture expanding, but provided the Chinese economy with profitable opportunities. When this was achieved, China would usually remove trade barriers on the specific good, which often yielded China a favorable status among the global economic world. This was often followed by currency devaluation, which gave China's now growing export industry an advantage over US export industry, and kept the cost of labor and price of Chinese goods cheaper and more likely to be consumed by the international market. China's joint ventures with foreign investors were set up with a VIE structure, which kept foreign investors from owning any of the company's assets, but allowed the foreign investors to reap profits or losses—via contractual agreements between the VIE(offshore shell company) and the Chinese company, which were not legally binding in China. This often tricked American investors into thinking that they owned an actual stake in the Chinese company, without seeing how China was guaranteed to reap most of the benefit. The Chinese, if they wanted, could then sabotage the company by restricting it from being transparent with their audits, which would lead to the SEC delisting the company, and thus causing investors to lose millions, with those Chinese investors who set up the VIE being able to keep much of the foreign investment. China has also orchestrated agreements with nations in central Africa, such as the Democratic Republic of Congo (DRC), in which China would agree to build roads, schools, and hospitals there in exchange for Chinese companies being allowed to mine mineral resources like cobalt and copper. Cobalt is one of the main components of lithium ion batteries which are used in electric vehicles and also in critical military equipment such as submarines, surface warships, jet fighters, surveillance aircraft, intelligence, surveillance, and reconnaissance systems, satellites, etc. Without cobalt, batteries would not have the self-cooling component that mitigates the chances of overheating and fires. And without an adequate supply chain of batteries, much of the nations' climate change efforts and more noteworthy their defense capabilities would be severely compromised. Because the Congo is sitting on 70% of the world's cobalt supply, the country has become a top attraction among nations looking to make the transition to electric vehicles. However, China has met criticism from the DRC president, whom in 2021 had called for a review of the contract concerning the multi billion dollar cobalt-for-infrastructure project originally established between China and the DRC in 2008. Thus far much of the funds have been more heavily prioritized to the mining projects, as opposed to the job creation/infrastructure projects that China agreed to help develop. The DRC has since kicked out or asked a number of Chinese-owned mining companies in the Congo to leave, believing that they have cheated the Congo out of money owed to them from the agreement to develop infrastructure in the DRC in exchange for mining cobalt, and also disregarded the environmental regulations of the DRC. Under the original agreement established in 2008, the DRC was to essentially barter its cobalt and copper minerals in exchange for China developing 9 billions dollars worth of infrastructure, which the DRC would agree to pay back at 0% interest rate. Over the years under pressure from the International Monetary Fund, whom is helping the Congo with its debt woes, China agreed to reduce the loan to 6 billion. China also canceled a small portion of the loan during the 2020 pandemic to help the DRC deal with the economic fallback from the COVID-19 crisis. Just as Saudi Arabia is the primary focus of energy production regarding oil, the Congo is the primary focus of production regarding electric power, as cobalt is the most critical element in battery manufacturing.

In March of 2022, Saudi Arabia was considering selling its oil to the Chinese in exchange for Chinese Yuan instead of US dollars. The consideration led to a brief spike in the value of the yuan. However, without a guarantee of military support from China, specifically in regards to the threat of Iran over Yemen, Saudi Arabia is unlikely to ratify such an oil deal with China. China's propensity for unfair dealings could also deter Saudi Arabia from ever seeking out security guarantees from China. All the while, Chinese mining companies being met with suspicion from the DRC would allow Russia to step in and possibly corner the cobalt market, which would give Russia a long term strategic advantage. Russia has forayed into central Africa in the hopes of securing mining contracts. One example is Russia's relations with the Central African Republic (CAR). In recent years, the Central African Republic(CAR) has been embroiled in civil unrest stemming from 2013 when President François Bozizé was overthrown. However, in 2016, Faustin-Archange Touadéra was elected President of the CAR, but has met consistent opposition from rebel groups situated in the country. Both Russia and France have sent troops to aid Touadera's government, but the CAR has found the Russian aid to be more successful in training CAR fighters to defend the government against the rebel militias. The deal established between Russia and the CAR was that in exchange for military support and training from Russia, the CAR would allow Russia to access its deposits of diamonds, gold and uranium. If Russia orchestrates a similar deal with the Democratic Republic of the Congo(DRC), Russia will attain access to 70% of the world's cobalt reserves, which would provide Russia considerable influence over China's battery manufacturing market and also the defense capabilities of most nations. China relies on the mineral cobalt to manufacture lithium ion batteries, while US defense relies on China's export of those batteries. Russia's invasion of Ukraine gives Russia access to eastern Ukraine's 500,000 tons of lithium oxide, which under the scenario that Russia secure a cobalt deal with the DRC, would allow Russia to usurp China as the lead supplier of lithium ion batteries. Combine this with the aforementioned possibility of Russia gaining control of the ethanol market by withholding fertilizer from the US, Russia thus becomes the global leader and supplier of the critical climate control resources: electric and bio-fuels. Such a prospect can be used to the advantage of the DRC. The Democratic Republic of Congo's president could begin a plan to integrate Russia in tandem with the already existing Chinese mining companies in the Congo and usher in a phase of Russian mining companies being allowed access to increasingly more of the Congo's cobalt reserves.... in a deal that would provide the DRC with military aid from Russia. A start would be expelling from the Congo the Chinese mining company "China Molybdenum", whom the DRC has already suspended from operating one of the world's largest cobalt mining sites, the Tenke Fungurume copper and cobalt mine. China Molybdenum was cited by the Congolese government for safety violations, not reporting cobalt and copper extraction totals, and also withholding royalties owed to the DRC from the mineral acquisitions. If the DRC expels the Chinese company and nationalizes the cobalt mine, they can offer the Tenke Fungurume copper and cobalt mining site to the Russians. Such a mining deal for Russia, however, would have to come with a major stipulation. The stipulation should be that Russia allow the President of the DRC to take a lead role in mediating for resolutions aimed to resolve Russia's geopolitical conflicts, with the eventual goal of persuading Russia to apply a fully diplomatic course of action. In exchange for being allowed serve as a major mediator of peace in eastern European geopolitical crises, the Congolese President would set up a deal that would allow Russia to access the Congo's cobalt mineral reserves in exchange for military support. In that scenario, with Russian and Chinese mining companies now extracting cobalt in the DRC, the DRC can pass a bill that would allow them to nationalize or hand over mining sites of companies engaged in unscrupulous practices. For example if a Chinese mining firm is committing various violations and abuses, the DRC can remove the company as an operator of the mining site and replace it with a Russian company. This infuses a competitive element in the mining industry within the DRC and should help deter abuses, cheating, and violations by foreign mining companies. This would also help ensure that the DRC gets its fair share of royalty payments and infrastructure development. Due to IMF aid, which the DRC is currently receiving in 2022, the DRC should be careful establishing mining deals with the Russians, as the IMF has already suspended the ceremonial role held by Russian representative, Aleksei Mozhin, over the Russian invasion of Ukraine. However, the fact that this deal with Russia is predicated on Congolese mediation in helping to resolve Russia's geopolitical conflicts, the IMF might not see this as a major issue affecting their loan agreement with the DRC.

Russia and China controlling the cobalt market would allow such nations to establish deterrence against aggressive and provocational western nations looking to interfere with domestic stability in eastern countries. In recent years, due to China's role in producing lithium ion batteries which the US depends on for its electric and defense capabilities, the US by default has had to maintain a careful approach in dealing with contentious issues regarding China's geopolitical agenda. It was either that or face the possibility of battery shortage if China would decide to withhold its battery exports from the US in retaliation for any US hostility towards China. Russia, on the other hand, had only been able to apply such leverage against Germany, whom had been reliant on

Russian oil, gas, and wheat exports. And for this reason, Germany had become more than compelled to apply conciliatory measures towards Russia in order to avoid upsetting this delicate arrangement, which if compromised would have systemic implications for the German economy. These dependencies are without question a deterrent to the aggressive militaristic and provocational approach since nations would prefer to maintain an accordance, resulting in a stable economy than to upset the balance by risking a war and an economic crisis. Under a cobalt deal between Russia, China, and the DRC, Russia would now be able to elicit a greater dependency from western nations that are reliant on lithium ion battery exports from the east. This dependency that would deter provocation and expansionary motives. The threat of Russia withholding cobalt exports to China in order to deter western hostility, would result in a decline in the amount of batteries that China can produce and export to the west. This would thus affect western nations, and also compel western nations to avoid cultivating hostilities with Russia since their choices in this case would be either diplomacy, or risk losing electric energy supplies. The importance of this cannot be understated because even in a future where the current geopolitical crisis between Russia and Ukraine eventually comes to an end, the west will still have its eye on the land that Russia sits upon, and will also seek to justify some form of incursion to try and separate Rus people from Rus lands in order to acquire the vast variety of resources and mineral deposits situated there. Lack of sufficient mineral resources in western Europe and the United States for the sake of maintaining their industrial efforts has been a factor leading to their need to interfere in mid-east, Latin American, African, and Russian geopolitics. Before Saudi Arabia was a proven oil-rich land, Russia had been the primary reservoir of oil and grain. Poland, France, Germany, Sweden have all historically either tried to invade or justify the military conquest of Russia for this very reason. Even when conflict broke out between western nations like England and France in 1812, Russia's export of grain to England during that time had become a flashpoint precipitating a French invasion of Russia. Germany's military incursions east towards Russia during World War I and II were largely motivated by acquiring access to Ukraine's grain production and Russia's oil, which Germany needed for sustaining its logistics, artillery and other military hardware. Germany could not produce enough oil or grain from their own land.

The DRC government not only needs training for its defense, but also arms and infrastructure since much of central Africa is marred by violence, corruption, and in-fighting. There are a number of rebel groups in the Congo that have been able to acquire weapons via the illegals arms export industry from various parts of the world.

However, some of the rebels have sought amnesty from the DRC and want to be integrated into its government forces. Germany should seek to establish an arms deal that coincides with the Congo's efforts to do just that—provide amnesty and integration of rebel groups into the DRC. However, Germany should buy the arms from Ukraine before shipping them to the DRC, which would help regulate sporadic arms dealing in the Congo and allow Ukraine to dominate the market and recover their economy. The training of DRC defense forces, however, should be conducted by Russian personnel. In exchange for an amnesty for arms deal between Germany and the Congo—which entails that if the DRC provides amnesty to rebel groups, Germany would supply arms to the DRC government via purchasing them from Ukraine—Germany would be allowed to build a dam in the Congo for green hydrogen development. Germany has been trying to transition to electric energy production using hydrogen, with a goal of mass producing hydrogen fuel cells for electric vehicles. Unlike lithium ion batteries, hydrogen fuel cells do not rely on cobalt. They are developed with platinum. Research, however, has found that cobalt can substitute platinum in hydrogen fuel cells and also lower the cost of production. Should Germany seek an option to use cobalt instead of platinum, they could simply purchase the cobalt from either the Chinese or Russian mining companies operating in the Congo. Furthermore, should Germany establish a deal with Saudi Arabia where Germany would agree to uphold Saudi Arabia's security in exchange for oil being traded in Euros or Deutschmarks, The DRC should set aside a volunteer group for the German army via a Congolese military base in Germany. This creates a supply chain of dependency where the DRC is reliant on training from Russia in exchange for offering cobalt mining contracts, arms from Germany who buys them from Ukrainian oligarchs which will help Ukraine's economy recover, and infrastructure from the Chinese in exchange for cobalt mining contracts. This leaves us with a new consortium of nations for world peace and stability: the Democratic Republic of the Congo, Russia, China, Ukraine, Germany, and Saudi Arabia.

Chapter 4: Russia's International Support

Coinciding with Germany's increasing engagement with Saudi Arabia, will be Russia's engagement with Latin America. During the Cold War, the Cuban Revolution in the 1950s provided a strategic framework for the Soviet Union's subversion of US security interests in the western hemisphere. Havana thus became ground zero for Moscow's efforts, and it was there that the Soviet Union established a military base. For a number of years, the Soviet Union provided direct military aid to Cuba via shipping arms to Havana. They also supported other leftist/anti-US regimes in Latin America during the Cold War. But when the Soviet Union collapsed in 1991, Moscow had reduced their presence and influence there, which ultimately took Russia off the radar of the US security apparatus. Nevertheless, the new Russian Federation inherited some of those Latin American/Soviet ties of the past, but at the same time, Russia was aware that any attempts to re-establish those Cold Era partnerships would require the type of arrangement that Russia would not be able to afford. And this was the case initially after the establishment of the Russian Federation in 1991. However, things would change in the late 1990s, when Russia would increase their engagement of Latin American countries and seek to forge greater cooperation, especially with those nations who were having contentious issues with the United States, one such being Columbia. Russia's support for Columbia's president at the time, Ernesto Samper, despite his ties to drug cartels, led to Columbia purchasing Russian military helicopters instead of US machinery. This move by Columbia was in breach of a deal in which Columbia agreed to purchase US-made equipment. Russia followed up by looking to establish—for its arms exports—a market in Latin America. Thus, Russia's trade relationship with Latin America increased, more specifically with countries like Brazil, Argentina, and Mexico. Still and all, it was largely less noteworthy than Russia's trade agreements with much of Europe, and Russia's ties with Latin America at this time in the late 1990s/early 2000s posed no security issue to the United States. Despite that being the case, many Latin American countries would become, nonetheless, more compelled, as a result of this Russian engagement of the region, to not only exert more defiance to US interests, but also seek to establish themselves more prominently on the international scene as major players in global affairs. Russia was further able to establish rapport with Latin American countries by way of their aloof-nees towards internal domestic policy within Latin American countries. Russia normally wouldn't question Cuba or Venezuela about human rights abuses, and Russia knew that those countries would not question them in a similar fashion. Since the 2000s, amid NATO's growing expansion eastward, Russia's

concurrent anti-Americanism and insistence on a multi-polar world order found resonance among leaders in Latin America. Hugo Chavez, Raul Castro, and Daniel Ortega were among Latin America's most Russia-friendly leaders. Russia's nostalgia movement, which glorified the era of Russia's past—from the Russian empire to the Soviet Union—coincided with Russia's engagement of Latin America which has its origins during the time of the Soviet Union when the Soviet Union set up a military base and ballistic missiles in Cuba in the 1960s. At the same time, those high ranking officials in Latin America who had fond memories of the Cold War era insurgencies there were welcoming of this desire to re-establish those close ties. They also knew that if such close ties were unattainable, they could still benefit financially from a cooperation with Russia. And this turned out to be the case. Cuba had its Soviet era debt canceled by the Russian Federation, and along with Nicaragua and Venezuela, received financial aid from Russia in exchange for recognizing Russia's policy within Russia's geopolitical sphere of influence in eastern Europe. Those Latin American countries recognized separatist regions in Georgia, and agreed to allow Russia to set up sovereign military bases in their countries at a future date. In 2014, Russia's defense Minister Sergei Shoigu announced Russia's plans to build military bases in Nicaragua, Cuba, and Venezuela, and much of this effort was motivated by US influence in the Ukraine crisis.

Back in 2011, Russian arms dealer Viktor Bout was convicted in the Unites States on four counts of conspiracy to sell antiaircraft weapons to Columbian terrorists for the purpose of using them against Americans. This was to the dismay of the Russian Federation, whom would accuse the US of violating international standards of arrest and detention. In retrospect, the engagement of Russia towards Latin America since 2000 and more ominously after 2010 has been for the purpose of dealing with US policy in eastern Europe, which has been a policy that largely ignored Russia's concerns. Even back in 1997, Boris Nemtsov, who was Russia's Deputy Prime Minister at the time, would state during a visit to Latin America that a Russian presence in Latin America could help Russia deter any US anti-Russian influence near Russia's borders. US support for Georgia and Ukraine in 2008 and 2014 respectively led to Russia scaling up its military cooperation with Nicaragua.

Russia's engagement in Latin America is not solely for the purpose of military and economics, but for promotional reasons. Russia has promoted their growing ties with Latin America to the Russian audience as something to be part and parcel of Russia's growing global influence and their audacious defiance of the United States, setting up military cooperation right in their backyard. However, after Russia's invasion of Ukraine in 2022, which had a negative impact on how Russians view the Kremlin, Russia may become more urged to establish media influence in foreign countries for the sake of mending their international reputation, and this could become more evident in Latin America. It is possible that Russia may seek to promote its culture abroad by persuading foreign countries to broadcast Russian TV or Russian media on their networks. Russia, in recent years, had certainly presented Latin American culture to the Russian public, and because of that, the Russian public is more aware of Latin America's importance to Russia. Russia has also established Spanish-langauge broadcasting division for its RT network. While based in Moscow, the RT Spanish channel has bureaus in Cuba, Venezuela, and Argentina. It can be expected that Russia's engagement of Latin America, following Russia's invasion of Ukraine on February 24, 2022—largely motivated by NATO expansion—will expand considerably along economic, military, and political lines, and will reach as far was Mexico. The growing Latin American population in Texas will pose a serious risk to America's geographical overlay as Russia will likely seek to instigate separatism there. With the aid of Critical Race Theory doctrines being spread in US schools, Russia may find it even easier to sow discord among Americans. Heightened Russian influence will also embolden nations in Latin America to exert more political assertiveness with less and less regard for US interests. Due to this developing situation in Latin America, security agencies like the US's CIA and Russia's FSB will increase their intelligence gathering operations there, leading to a very intense intelligence and subversion war as American sentiment in Latin America will become of grave concern for the US amid a diplomatic tug or war between the US and Russia for the support of Latin American leaders. Much like Ukraine was the ultimate goal of NATO in Eastern Europe for the sake of cementing US dominance over Russia, Texas will be the ultimate goal and primary focal point of Russia's intention to destabilize the United States and end its unipolar moment. Russia will look to achieve this goal by slowly making their way from Latin America.

Western outrage and sanctions imposed upon Russia will likely only have a short term effect on the Russian state. In fact, the residual effects of the Russian invasion of Ukraine will in the long run more negatively impact the international economic standing of the United States. It has been clear that even throughout the Russia/Ukraine war, many nations have been apprehensive about excoriating or confronting Russia about its full-scale invasion of its foremost western neighbor, Ukraine. A good portion of these reluctant countries are in fact US allies. The nations which declare an almost unconditional backing of Russia since the invasion of Ukraine have been Syria, Belarus, Eritrea, North Korea, Cuba and Venezuela. Other countries like China have taken a conciliatory approach, choosing not to refer to Russia's military incursion of Ukraine as an "invasion." China has also refused to participate in widespread western efforts to sanction Russia. Much of this trepidation among nations to enact reprisals against Russia is largely due in part to their economic and military ties to Russia. Russia has been able to use their vast resources of oil, arms, and defense to secure strategic partnerships. Because of this, Russia may have a lifeline to escape any long term impact of the economic constraints levied upon them by the west. Russia is paying close attention to those nations that have benefited from Russian ties, but considers China as its most critical partner who can mitigate the damage that sanctions will trigger. Many consider China's strong ties to Russia as a possible catalyst towards productive peace talks between Russia and Ukraine with China as a mediator.

Russia provides 60 percent of India's military artillery, as the byproduct of a relationship that spans decades. For this reason, India has declined to engage in provocative rhetoric about Russia's war in Ukraine, and has also encouraged for a peaceful solution to the crisis. They also applied this approach after Russia's annexation of Crimea in 2014. There are certain implication for India that would come with ostracizing Russia, implications that India is not prepared to encounter in the near term. India has attempted to wean itself from its arms reliance on Russia by pursuing arms deals with other nations, but has nevertheless remained reliant on Russia in this regard. Such has been imperative due to the hostility India has encountered from Pakistan and China, which is why India is very eager about measures that could end the Russia/Ukraine war. In the meantime, India's central bank is considering a trade agreement with Russia that would involve the exclusive use of Indian rupees and rubles for transactions. India also continues to buy Russian oil and gas and is looking to set up a deal in which India would buy 3 million barrels of oil from Russia at a discount.

Israel is another country that has been reluctant to impose sanctions against Russia since it is in their law that they could only apply sanctions against a country that has been anathematized to be an enemy to Israel. Israel has also vowed not to supply arms to Ukraine, and refuses to sell pegasus spyware to NATO members. However, Israel has volunteered to mediate peace between Russia and Ukraine, as Israel's Prime Minister has spoken to both the Russian president Vladimir Putin and Ukrainian President Volodymyr Zelenskyy. Much of Israel's cautios approach towards Russia has to do with Russia's presence in Syria as an ally to the Assad government, and the fact that Russia has allowed Israel's air force to conduct strikes on Iran bases stationed in Syria. Iran stores arms on Syrian soil and ships them to Hezbollah in Lebanon and militia groups in Yemen and the Gaza strip. In being allowed to

access Syrian airspace, Israel can better protect their own national security. In this regard, Russia is a critical ally for the state of Israel, and the biggest gain that Russia can acquire in relation to Israel is media support that could combat western propaganda which has largely painted Russia as a longstanding threat to the United States and the world since World War II. As a stand-between between Israel and Iran/Shiite and Sunni sectarianism, Russia will be able to garner considerable media aid from the likes of reputable and renown news outlets such as the Jerusalem Post and Al Jazeera, both of which will become central to the reporting of global affairs.

Saudi Arabia and OPEC member countries have also remained keen to avoid condemning Russia for the invasion of Ukraine. Saudi Arabia and OPEC consider Russia as a critical ally in the regulation of global oil prices. In 2019, OPEC invited Russia to be part of an expanded network called "OPEC+" to help facilitate cost-efficient and profitable oil output for the purpose of countering the American shale oil boom. Since the Russian invasion of Ukraine, Saudi Arabia has refused requests by the US to increase oil output in order to combat the rise of oil prices that came about as a result of sanctions and the oil embargoes against Russia. Thus Saudi Arabia has indicated that hey are unwilling to compromise the strategic partnership between OPEC and Russia on global oil output.

While Turkey has condemned the Russian invasion of Ukraine, they have refused to sanction or cut off Russia's access to their airspace. Turkey's considers Russia's presence in Syria as a deterrent to the development of a possible Kurdish state near Turkey's border. Turkey has also purchased s-400 anti-aircraft missiles from Russia and set up energy contracts. Still and all, Turkey remains intent on navigating all sides of the conflict. Despite their ties with Russia, Turkey has delivered Turkish made drones to Ukraine, which have helped Ukraine resist the Russian invasion.

South Africa has openly blamed NATO for the war in Ukraine and refused to condemn Russia. For South Africa, their perspective is heavily rooted in a backdrop going back to the Cold War era when the Soviet Union backed anti-apartheid activists in South Africa, while the United States would maintain their support for the apartheid regime for a number of years.

Chapter 5: The First Non-Aggression Pact

It is quite often pointed out that because NATO is applying the same restraint towards Russia after Russia's invasion of Ukraine that France and England applied towards Germany after Germany invaded of Poland in 1939, the result will somehow be the same—just as Hitler became emboldened to embark upon an imperialist agenda, Putin will likely try the same approach. In 1939, France was hoping to deter German aggression by mobilizing near the Franco/German border along the Maginot line, much in the way NATO thinks it could deter Russian aggression by mobilizing its troops near the border within each NATO member country. This approach certainly didn't work then and many believe it will not work in the case of Russia's intentions after their invasion of Ukraine. In retrospect, France could have invaded Germany before Hitler decided to strike first, but that would require coming off as the aggressor, not really knowing at that time that Hitler was planning to take over the world and kill 6 million Jews. But in hindsight, striking first certainly may have stopped Hitler. Another factor in Hitler's decision to expand his military operations was due to the fact that after Germany invaded Poland, both France and England declared war on Germany. In this regard, Hitler had every reason to believe that both nations would eventually attempt to stifle or attack Germany. In contrast, no onlooking nations as of March 27, 2022 have formally declared war on Russia because of Russia's invasion of Ukraine. Of course, there is another aspect that can be called into question in terms how the invasion may be sowing the seeds of a greater conflict. That aspect pertains to how sanctions are isolating Russia from the international economy, much like the Treaty of Versailles isolated Germany from the international economy. And it is quite similar how both economic restrictions uphold a constraint which ultimately keeps the nation from compensating for previous malfeasance and also paying their debts to recipients who are removed from the nation's foreign policy mishaps. After World War I, Germany had trouble paying reparations and debts because their access to economic revenue was cut off. At the same time, Russia, even if they would oblige, could not pay reparations if their revenue stream is cut off. In March of 2022, after heavy sanctions were levied upon them, Russia had to scrape up much of its US dollar holdings in order to meet its Eurobond obligation. Eurobonds are offshore bonds denominated in hard currency, usually US dollars, that nations can issue in order to raise money. Had Russia not stockpiled US currency, they would have not been able to meet that obligation and many investors who are far removed from Russian policy making would have incurred serious losses. This draws upon a very valid question; can financial

constraints be applied in such a way that the nation under condemnation would be punished economically, not to the point where it cannot meet the very obligations that those constraints put into place. Lets consider the famous economist John Maynard Keynes. John Maynard Keynes was in attendance at the Paris Conference, but left abruptly in protest of the treaty, which he felt was counter-intuitive and setting the stage for further conflict in Europe. In his book, The Economic Consequences of the Peace, which was published in December 1919, Keynes was adamant that the stiff penalties imposed by the Treaty of Versailles upon Germany after World War I would lead to the economic collapse of the country, and thus give rise to geopolitical unrest. In the fall of 1918, it had become very clear that Germany was unlikely to win the Great War(WWI). Germany had become depleted militarily after 4 years of attacks, and could no longer resist the onslaught of allied forces, which had been reinforced by US entry into World War I. In order to circumvent a catastrophic outcome for Germany, the German government reached out to US President Woodrow Wilson in October of 1918, and requested that he help set up an armistice agreement. President Woodrow Wilson had earlier that year laid out a peace accordance called Fourteen Points and the League of Nations, which was a proposal outlining how post-war recovery should be approached by the nations of the world. Germany had requested that the armistice follow along the lines of Wilson's Fourteen Points, which included *1. Open covenants of peace, openly arrived at, after which there shall be no private international understandings of any kind, but diplomacy shall proceed always frankly and in the public view. 2. Absolute freedom of navigation upon the seas, outside territorial waters, alike in peace and in war, except as the seas may be closed in whole or in part by international action for the enforcement of international covenants. 3. The removal, so far as possible, of all economic barriers and the establishment of an equality of trade conditions among all the nations consenting to the peace and associating themselves for its maintenance. 4. Adequate guarantees given and taken that national armaments will be reduced to the lowest points consistent with domestic safety. 5. A free, open-minded and absolutely impartial adjustment of all colonial claims based upon a strict observance of the principle that in determining all such questions of sovereignty, the interests of the populations concerned must have equal weight with the equitable claims of the government whose title is to be determined. 6. The evacuation of all Russian territory and such a settlement of all questions affecting Russia as will secure the best and freest cooperation of the other nations of the world in obtaining for her an unhampered and unembarrassed opportunity for the independent determination of*.

her own political development and national policy and assure her of a sincere welcome into the society of free nations under institutions of her own choosing; and, more than a welcome, assistance also of every kind that she may need and may herself desire. The treatment accorded Russia by her sister nations in the months to come will be the acid test of their goodwill, of their comprehension of her needs as distinguished from their own interests, and of their intelligent and unselfish sympathy. 7. Belgium, the whole world will agree, must be evacuated and restored without any attempt to limit the sovereignty which she enjoys in common with all other free nations. No other single act will serve as this will serve to restore confidence among the nations in the laws which they have themselves set and determined for the government of their relations with one another. Without this healing act the whole structure and validity of international law is forever impaired. 8. All French territory should be freed and the invaded portions restored, and the wrong done to France by Prussia in 1871 in the matter of Alsace-Lorraine, which has unsettled the peace of the world for nearly fifty years, should be righted in order that peace may once more be made secure in the interest of all. 9. A readjustment of the frontiers of Italy should be effected along clearly recognizable lines of nationality. 10. The people of Austria-Hungary, whose place among the nations we wish to see safeguarded and assured, should be accorded the freest opportunity of autonomous development. 12. The Turkish portions of the present Ottoman Empire should be assured a secure sovereignty, but the other nationalities which are now under Turkish rule should be assured an undoubted security of life and an absolutely unmolested opportunity of autonomous development; and the Dardanelles should be permanently opened as a free passage to the ships and commerce of all nations under international guarantees. 13. An independent Polish state should be erected which should include the territories inhabited by indisputably Polish populations, which should be assured a free and secure access to the sea, and whose political and economic independence and territorial integrity should be guaranteed by international covenants. 14. A general association of nations must be formed under specific covenants for the purpose of affording mutual guarantees of political independence and territorial integrity to great and small [states] alike.

On November 11, 1918, the US would comply with Germany's request and an armistice established along the lines of the Fourteen Points was signed and effectuated, ending the fighting in World War I.

In January 1919, John Maynard Keynes attended the Paris Peace Conference as a representative of the British Treasury, having

become well-known for his brilliance in financial strategy. During the conference, he sat on the economic council as an advisor to British Prime Minister David Lloyd George. Much of the conference's decision making authority would be wielded by President Wilson, Prime Minister Lloyd George, and French Prime Minister Georges Clemenceau. Germany was not given any role in the conference, which ultimately left their fate in the hands of the aforementioned allied countries. Shortly after the conference convened, it became apparent that the treaty would be very different from the previous armistice settled between Germany and the US back in November of 1918. Wilson caved in to mounting pressure from France, who was seeking revenge for the constraints levied upon them previously by Germany after the Franco Prussian war in 1871 under the Treaty of Frankfurt. Lloyd George tried to remain neutral, but ultimately sided with France and agreed that Germany be forced to pay reparations for damages to civilian life and property in Allied countries. The Treaty of Versailles blamed Germany entirely for World War I, and forced Germany to cover the damages to allied countries, and at the same acquitted Allied countries from having to pay for damages they inflicted to German civilians. The treaty was designed to crush Germany, take away 10% of their territory, disarm them, restrict their access to maritime trade, confiscate their foreign financial reserves and merchant carrier fleet. All of this was topped with a 30+ billion US dollar reparations obligation that Germany was required to pay, with a stipulation that if they didn't, the Allies would be in their right to invade the country. This horrified Keynes, who offered a plan in which Germany would be granted a loan for basic items as they work on making reparation payments. Lloyd George approved of this proposal, but Woodrow Wilson believed that it would be rejected by Congress. Keynes, who was extremely disappointed with Wilson's explanation, resigned from his role at the Paris conference. Germany, at first, refused to agree to these terms, but ultimately gave in as the Allies set up a food blockade of Germany, which forced Germany to sign the treaty.

As expected, Germany shortly thereafter fell behind on their reparation payments, and in 1923, France and Belgium forces occupied the industrial Ruhr region as accorded by the Treaty of Versailles, which stated that the Allies could invade if Germany falls back on its reparation payments. At the time, part of the reparation payments were to be paid by Germany in the form of coal exports to France, Belgium and Italy annually for a period of 10 years. This incursion by French and Belgium forces was met with protests by German workers, who would close down factories in the Ruhr region. The result of this led to extreme inflation, which led to Germany's economic collapse in November of 1923. This gave way to the rise of the Nazi party led by Adolf Hitler, who would launch an

unsuccessful coup against the German government for signing the Treaty of Versailles. Over the years, however, with the help of the Dawes plan which declared that America would provide loans to the German government, Germany's 132 billion gold mark reparation debt was agreed to be reduced to 36 billion. In 1932, payments were suspended altogether to help Germany recover from the global financial crisis. Later, Hitler, would take power in Germany and undermine the treaty altogether, as the damage from the Treaty of Versailles had already been done, and Germany's subsequent re-militarization in defiance of the treaty's disarmament requirement for Germany was already in full swing, set to bring the world into another war.

If we fast-foward to the present circumstances of 2022 in which Russia and Ukraine is embroiled in a military conflict, we can see that there is some distinction and similarities in the backdrop that led to World War II and the backdrop that led to the Russian invasion of Ukraine. For instance, Germany's primary motive was to regain the territories ceded by Germany when they signed the Treaty of Versailles. Those territories were Belgium, Czechoslovakia, Poland, Alsace and Lorraine, and overseas colonies in China, Pacific and Africa. If we figure that re-expansion imperialistic motive into Putin's outlook, one would have to argue that Putin has a desire to revive the Soviet Union, which would require invading or annexing not only Ukraine, but also Armenia, Azerbaijan, Belarus, Estonia, Georgia, Kazakhstan, Kyrgyzstan, Latvia, Lithuania, Moldova, Tajikistan, Turkmenistan, and Uzbekistan. In contrast to this similarity, the distinction would be that the catalyst behind Hitler's desire to reclaim lost territories was largely rooted in the Treaty of Versailles, which decreed that Germany relinquish much of its territories. Putin, on the other hand, was motivated by the prospect of a foremost western neighbor joining a multi-national military bloc(NATO) that could supply it with nuclear weapons which could be aimed at Russia. In fact this was a flash-point for Russia's policy against Ukraine since 2014. It is possible that this revolting prospect could have motivated pro-Soviet era nostalgia that was used to justify the Russian annexation of Crimea in 2014. Crimea was a gift to Ukraine from the Soviet Union General Secretary Nikita Khrushchev in 1954, a transfer that the Russian Federation tried to delegitimize. Unlike Germany, Russia was not under any serious longstanding financial constraints, that is, until after Russia invaded Ukraine in February of 2022. In this regard, we could compare Russia's invasion of Ukraine to Germany's military operations in World War I, with the ensuing reprisals against Germany under the Treaty of Versailles being akin to the international sanctions levied upon Russia after their invasion of Ukraine in 2022. Even in this case, the response to such sanctions by Russia may not mirror

completely, Germany's response to the Treaty of Versailles. Russia is not being required to pay reparations to Ukraine nor being mandated to export resources to multiple nations. In fact, the opposite is being applied. Russia's export markets are being stifled by embargoes, and Russia is not facing the threat of invasion if unable to make good on any sort of financial obligation levied upon them. Their military will also remain fully intact should they withdraw their forces from Ukraine, unlike Germany's after WWI, which was considerably reduced and rendered ineffective. This is why Russia's post-sanction approach may differ from Germany's post-Treaty of Versailles approach. If anything, sanctioning Russia is putting Germany back into an economic desperation that led to its assertive and defiant policies throughout the 1930's, which will much like Germany of the 1930s, compel Germany of the 2020s and beyond to remove all constraints placed upon them by western allies and take the same course of action the Nazis took in terms of re-militarization and self-determination, which is why this book foresees the euro usurping the US dollar as the world's reserve currency.

Russia and Germany's financial ties since World War I have been marked by periods of tension and harmony. After World War I, both nations found it rather easy to revert back to normalized trade relations, as the post-war period allowed both sides to prioritize their respective domestic problems. Within 3 years after the war ended, Russia(Soviet Union) and Germany signed the treaty of Rapallo in 1922. Even as Hitler came to power 11 years later with an anti-Bolshevik and anti-Russian platform, Germany and Russia nevertheless retained a cohesive trade relationship which gave Germany the much needed resources to remilitarize and launch an offensive against Poland in 1939. The economic arrangement between Germany and Russia led to the establishment of a Nazi-Soviet non-aggression pact in which the Soviets would take Poland from the east, while Germany would take Poland via west. This pact was later broken by Hitler, setting off World War II.

German and Russian relations just prior to the war were imperative to the national security and military apparatus of each nation. Thus the ratification of the German-Russian non-aggression pact allowed Germany to protract its military operations, and at the same time ease Russia's fear of a German invasion of the Soviet Union. Such was carefully crafted by Hitler, who used Germany's trade relationship with Russia to gain the trust that would buy him time and prevent Germany from starting a two-front war upon invading Poland. He also needed Russia's valuable raw materials to sustain the German war machine. These goals could only be achieved by establishing both a political and economic accordance. Thus Germany and Russia would sign a trade agreement, which fostered the German war effort throughout much of the 1940s when Germany was invading much of western and central Europe. This economic agreement normalized relations between the Soviet Union and Germany and was more integral to the German war effort than the non-aggression pact was. It is often proposed amongst academic scholarship that had France and England attacked Germany sooner after declaring war against Germany in 1939, the devastation from World War II could have been avoided. But we see in World War I, how the overlay supports the Napoleonic course of action regarding France's 1812 invasion of Russia, embarked upon because Russia was providing grain to England, whom the French were at war with. So in this fabric, one has to ask about France and England's outlook on Russia's empowerment of the German War machine by way of their export of raw materials to Germany, and if a course of action against Russia before 1941 would have been warranted by the Allied Powers. And does this perspective justify comparing Putin moreso to Napoleon than to Hitler since Putin's insistence on expansion would follow along the lines of Napoleon's—for the sake of cutting off another country's exports to an adversarial nation.

After Hitler rose to power in Germany, his ideological attacks on Bolshevism and Germany's subsequent break in political relations with Russia did not affect the overall standing of trade between Germany and Russia, even as Hitler tried to establish economic independence in Germany, encouraging policies that would force Germany to try and rely on their own resources for the sake of self-sufficiency, so that Germany would not require the imports from foreign nations during times of war. When this goal was discovered to be unfeasible, Germany strengthened their economic ties with the Soviet Union. In 1936, despite Nazi policy against communism and Bolshevism, Germany and the Soviet Union established a credit agreement which further consolidated their trade relationship. It provided Germany greater access to Russia's raw materials such as metals and oil. This proved vital to Hitler rearmament program since it was the case that before this agreement was established, Germany lacked the sufficient materials to sustain the arms effort. And it is likely that this may have been a source of resentment for the Nazis because without Russia, Germany could neither be economically self-sufficient nor militarily adept in terms of deploying its advanced weaponry. The 1936 credit agreement with Russia gave Germany the necessary tools for mobilization. In 1938, both Germany and the Soviet Union would review their economic circumstances. All in all, the establishment of this credit agreement would highlight a serious dichotomy between Nazi Germany's ideological framework and their foreign policy, which provides some backdrop to the bemusement that has arisen upon observation at how western nations have been able to condemn

Russia for the invasion of Ukraine in 2022, but nonetheless continue to buy their oil and gas. This inconsistency has been a staple of geopolitics for quite some time, and was applied even during World War II. Furthermore, it was likely that the inconsistency and downright contradiction between Germany's foreign policy and their ideological dogma cultivated a growing mistrust between the two nations despite the sustained economic arrangement. Perhaps the arrest of thousands of ethnic Germans living in Russia immediately proceeding Hitler's invasion of Poland could have been the impetus that set Germany on the course to breaking the non-aggression pact. We see this aspect of ethnic oppression influencing the policy of the Russian federation against Chechnya in 1999, Georgia in 2008, and Ukraine in 2014. The backdrop of those conflicts revolved around the treatment of Russian minorities in those countries. It is likely that Stalin's treatment of ethnic Germans in Russia in 1939 may have set Germany on a path against Russia.

Russia's raw material exports to Germany propped up Germany's ability to impose their will against western powers. It modernized Germany's military technology and gravely threatened the security of western and central European nations, as Hitler would often reinforce the need for living space. Germany's growing military stature and Hitler's rhetoric compelled nations like Great Britain and France to insist on taking a conciliatory approach in order to appease Germany. This was a far cry from their antipathy to the German state after World War I. We may see this played out between Russia and the United States, where the US after having embarked upon an antagonistic policy towards Russia since the Cold War, will be more compelled to apply conciliatory measures towards the Russian state after witnessing its bold aggression against Ukraine in 2022.

The conciliatory efforts applied by France and Britain towards Germany was never more apparent than at the 1938 Munich conference, where Hitler insisted on Germany's right to control the Sudetenland in Czechoslovakia because of the number of ethnic Germans residing there. This is very similar to Russia's justification for annexation of nearby countries in eastern Europe post Soviet-era —the fact that a significant number of ethnic Russians resided in those areas. At the 1938 Munich conference, Hitler argued that a prerequisite for uniting Germans in the region and thus ensuring adequate living space would be through annexing the Sudetenland into Germany. This, Hitler asserted, would aid his goal of Lebensraum. In response, France and Britain practiced what is called appeasement, essentially allowing Hitler to expand without intervention on the part of France or Britain. After Hitler annexed the Sudetenland, British Prime Minister Neville Chamberlain came under scrutiny for this approach, which he argued was for the sake of strategy—giving France and Britain time to mobilize and prepare for military conflict.

Moreso than easing tension between Germany and its western counterparts, the Munich Conference provided an impetus to greater trade ties between the Soviet Union and Germany. Neither France or Britain sought any input from the Soviet Union on Germany's annexation of the Sudetenland, which would have fostered more solidarity among France, Britain, and the Soviet Union, at least early enough to influence Germany's policy. But since the Soviet Union was left out, most likely because of how communism was viewed not just by Germany, but all of the west, Stalin decided that because of western appeasement towards Germany, the Soviet Union would be left alone in the event that Germany invade the country. So he decided to pursue a plan of improving political relations with Germany for the sake of delaying or even deterring outright aggression from Germany. As Germany began to acquire lands eastward, Hitler came to the conclusion that it would be in Germany's best interest to ally itself with Russia. This rapprochement between Germany and the Soviet Union allowed them to re-certify their economic ties after the Credit Agreement of 1936 expired in 1938. The arrangement allowed both nations to operate ideologically separate but economically entangled. As the Germans would continue their rearmament movement by acquiring raw materials from the Soviet Union, the Soviet Union in turn was able to benefit through access to Germany's military technologies. Back in 1920s, the Soviet Union secretly provided facilities to the Germans so that the Germans could build and test their arms developments in the Soviet Union in exchange for permitting the Soviet Union to access the blueprints for those technologies. In retrospect, western antipathy towards Russia has both exacerbated geopolitical issues and also curtailed potential solutions. We see this in the case of both the Munich conference and the Manhattan project, where in both cases, shunning Russia exacerbated the dangers arising from both the German war machine and later nuclear arms proliferation. This leads one to justify an argument that learning from history might involve early correspondence and input from Russia, as opposed to antagonism and provocation.

The diplomatic negotiations between Germany and the Soviets in 1938 and 1939 trod along a rocky road as both nations maintained a certain amount of distrust. The economic negotiations were conduced primarily by General Freidrich Schulenburg, who was the German Ambassador to the Soviet Union; Herr Karl Schnurre, the head of the Eastern European division of the Foreign Ministry; German Foreign Minister Joachim von Ribbentrop; Soviet Chargé of Affairs Georgi Astakov; and Viacheslav Molotov, the Soviet Prime Minister. Schulenberg sent a memo to the German Foreign Office, outlining a plan to extend the trade agreement through 1939. The extension gave Germany continued access to Russia's raw materials. Nevertheless, even after being left out of the Munich Conference, the Soviets continued to reach out to western powers, which likely kept the agreement from being further extended beyond 1939. As Karl Schnurre, the head of the Eastern European division of the Foreign Ministry was slated to travel to Moscow on January 20, 1939 to discuss the future of Soviet/Germany trade relations, his trip was suddenly canceled, and this had a negative impact on possible resolutions in the near term. Diplomats both on the German and Russian side believed that the other had some pretentious political agenda, and both sides insisted that political concessions be made before economic talks could resume. The Germans were suspicious of the Soviet Union's discourse with western powers. Nevertheless, the German diplomats continued reassuring the Soviet Union of their sincerity to continue with rapprochement and even agreed to see to it that anti-Bolshevik rhetoric would cease in Germany. Viacheslav Molotov, the Soviet Prime Minister, was concerned about Germany's motives and wanted Germany to run political negotiations concurrent with economic talks, and the German diplomats were adamant about gaining the trust of the Soviets. So this brief ospolitik measure of curbing anti-communist rhetoric in Germany was intended to satisfy Molotov's political demands. However, Schulenburg was concerned that the Soviets could use the political proposals to leverage Soviet talks with the western powers. This double-dealing aspect by the Soviet Union wore on Germany's ability to keep the Soviets interested in maintaining a trade and economic agreement. Nonetheless, German diplomats continued to urge the Soviet Union to make accordance with them on an economic agreement. But the Soviets, regardless, remained insistent on political bases being established. In June of 1939, Soviet Chargé Astakov met with Herr Dragonoff, the Bulgarian Minister, to discuss a potential non-aggression pact with Germany. The German foreign office, after being informed about the meeting, began putting together details for the pact. A meeting between Schnurre, Foreign Office Official Walther Schmidt, and Astakov and Evgeny Babarin, the head of the Soviet Trade Delegation, was called on July 24, 1939. At the meeting, Schnurre proposed a number of ways that Germany and the Soviet Union could establish an accordance. First, was through prioritizing a formal agreement to establish economic contracts, which he felt would cultivate better political associations. The second way to go about this, as Schnurre would assert, would be to normalize relations, which had already been underway prior to the meeting, as both nations attempted to discontinue the provocative rhetoric. The third step, Shnurre pointed out, was a complete effort to establish a meaningful political concordat. Even

though Schnurre appeared to fulfill Molotov's request and ease his concerns with those proposals, the Soviet Union still remained apprehensive about accepting the plan. The Soviets were steadfast in opting to continue relations with both Germany and the western powers. By July 28th, however, the Soviets decided to accept Schnurre's plan for German/Soviet accordance. Molotov wrote to Soviet Chargé Astakov: *"Political relations between the USSR and Germany may improve, of course, with an improvement in economic relations...if the Germans are sincerely changing course and really want to improve political relations with the USSR, they are obliged to state what this improvement represents in concrete terms...we would, of course, welcome any improvement in political relations between the two countries."*

Despite Molotov's statement, the Soviet Union continued to navigate diplomatically between Germany and the western powers for the purposes of ensuring Soviet security against a potential German attack. For this very reason, the German representatives had become anxiety-ridden about confirming an economic and political accordance with the Soviet Union. Hitler had already laid out his plans to attack Poland and wanted to confirm that the Soviet Union would not intervene. It was likely that the lack of certainty about this from Germany's end was due to Soviet oscillation between Germany and the western powers. This may have been one of the major factors that led to Hitler breaking the non-aggression pact in 1941, believing that because the Soviets were corresponding with the west, the west would persuade the Soviet Union to intervene against Germany. A non-aggression pact was of such deep concern to Hitler that he would send Foreign Minister von Ribbentrop to conference with Astakov on August 3rd 1939. Ribbentrop ensured Astakov at this meeting that Germany would expound on the details of the pact if the Soviet Union confirm their intent to establish a relationship with Germany. He asserted that the pact could only be successful if both sides were equally committed, and he also insisted that the Soviet Union cut ties with the west, along with the Soviets promising not to get involved in Germany's affairs. Once again, the Soviet government stalled on providing a decision to the German representatives, and continued to corroborate with the western powers. An Anglo-French delegation met with the Soviet government on August 10th, 1939 to discuss the future of Soviet/western relations. When the talks yielded little to no results, the Soviet Union pivoted back to Germany and confirmed a desire to officially establish a pact with the German state. Schnurre and Astakov met a number of times in Moscow to lay out the tenets of the contract as it related to the economic accordance. Ribbentrop and Molotov would put together the components of the non-aggression pact. Molotov continued to express the need for certain contingencies that would

have to be met for the agreement to work. He believed that Germany and the Soviet Union needed to confirm a trade and credit agreement, a non-aggression pact, and the establishment of a secret file that would outline the interests and expectations of each nation. By August 16th 1939, Germany stated that it was ready to sign a non-aggression pact after the conclusion of an economic agreement. Subsequently, on August 19th, Schnurre and Babarin would sign the economic portion of the agreement in Berlin. The agreement extended the trade relationship initiated by the Credit Agreement of 1936 up unto the mid-1940s and also increased exponentially the amount of goods to be traded. The contract laid out the terms of what each side was expected to contribute, terms which were largely unequal, as the Soviet Union was to provide a higher portion of goods than Germany. The Soviet Union was allocated 200 million Reichsmarks for the purpose of acquiring those goods which were agreed upon. While this credit seemed at first glance to favor the Soviet Union, all it did was offset the debt accrued by the Soviets under the 1936 Credit Agreement, which totaled 200 million Reichsmarks. The treaty nonetheless allowed the Soviet Union to trade their raw materials to Germany in exchange for German machinery and arms, which strengthened the capabilities of the Red Army and also helped reverse a declining Soviet industrial economy. In this sense, both sides enjoyed a mutual benefit of improving their respective arms industry. In other aspects, the Germans benefited to a significant degree since they were able to trade outdated machinery for vital raw materials from the Soviet Union. The outdated technology were often weapons used in World War I, along with coal exports. Germany was also allocated 200 million Reichsmarks to purchase Soviet goods. The economic deal allowed Germany to attain materials that Germany lacked on its own soil, materials such as oil, iron, food, lumber, cotton, and manganese, all of which were used to develop and enhance the German industrial economy and war machine. Despite having to trade away manufactured goods and hardware, Germany retained much of the advantage from the agreement. Bartering was the primary vehicle for trade under this pact since removing the necessity of hard currency allowed for a more efficient transfer of materials, and allowed Germany to designate the hard currency for other aspects of Germany's re-militarization program. Despite the advantages Germany attained from this agreement, German representatives continued to press the Soviet Union for more concessions, such as a delayed payment schedule in exchange for Germany helping the Soviet Union build factories in the Soviet Union over a term of 5 years. Thus new negotiations would take place between October 3rd 1939 and February 1940. The aftermath of these meetings led to a railway agreement between Germany and the Soviet Union, and provided a means for Germany to evade Britain's blockade of German goods, while also allowing Germany to increase the amount of goods it could trade with the Soviet Union. This new arrangement provided to Germany an increased amount of oil, cotton, phosphates, iron, platinum, and lumber. The Soviet Union, under this agreement, agreed to purchase for Germany other materials and metals from foreign countries. In this regard, the Soviet Union was acting as a third party buyer for Germany and thereby providing them access to foreign markets which Germany had been restricted from participating in. Moreover, a new payment schedule was agreed upon, one which allowed Germany to repay the Soviet Union for deliveries over a 27 month period. Paying the Soviet Union at a later date enabled Germany to spend more money on advancing their arms technology and war machinery.

Shortly after the signing of the economic agreement, the non-aggression pact was signed on August 23, 1939 in Moscow. This agreement, in contrast to the economic agreement, was publicly advertised to show the nature of the relationship between Germany and the Soviet Union. The non-aggression pact was not intended to be an alliance, but only an agreement in which both sides would decide to remain neutral if the other was attacked. Such a measure was applied to mitigate the chances of military conflict between the Soviet Union and Germany. The non-aggression pact was designed to last 25 years. A third aspect of the German/Soviet accordance was the formulation of classified file which would detail how Germany and the Soviet Union would allocate their respective spheres of influence. This provided a buffer zone between Germany and the Soviet Union and further reduced the chances of hostilities between both nations. The Secret Protocol, as it was called, is what led to the Soviet invasion of eastern Poland and the German invasion of western Poland. The ratification of the non-aggression pact prevented Hitler from starting a two-front war, as adhering to the Secret Protocol placed the area of Poland invaded by Germany in September of 1939 under the jurisdiction of Germany, leaving the rest of Poland under the jurisdiction of the Soviet Union. This would ease Stalin's concerns about a German invasion of the Soviet Union, and at the same time provide Germany access to the Soviet Union's raw materials. It is certainly arguable that had Stalin did the opposite—cut ties with Germany in the late 1930s and maintain a correspondence with the western powers, the Soviet Union may have attacked Germany after Germany would have invaded Poland, and thus prevented the escalation that occurred during World War II. Another factor in the case of Soviet alienation of Germany would be a far less extensive arsenal of weapons in the hands of the German war machine, owed to the fact that such an arsenal was contingent on Soviet export of its raw materials to Germany. Germany, without importing oil from the Soviet Union, would not have been able to develop its armaments, nor sustain its war effort since planes, tanks, and other components of mechanized warfare require adequate oil availability. Germany has never been self-sufficient when it came to oil production, for they could only provide 33% of their domestic need, never-mind military needs. Without Soviet oil, the German army could not conduct blitzkrieg nor fight for prolonged periods of time. Hence why access to Russian oil was critical to Germany's sustenance militarily and domestically. This has not changed even as of 2022, as roughly 98% of oil consumed in Germany is imported. 34% of those imports come from Russia.

The other critical material that the Soviet Union supplied to Germany was metal, which came in the form of pig iron, chrome, and manganese. These enabled Germany to develop a hardened steel framework for the various weapons and artillery they had in their arsenal. Prior to World War II, 65% of Germany's iron was imported. Minerals such as chrome, manganese, and steel were normally obtained from South Africa, but after Britain formed a blockade to deny Germany's access to those minerals, Germany was left having to rely on Russia. The lack of metals and iron in Germany made it imperative that Germany orchestrate trade deals with the Soviet Union. Without such, Germany would not have been able to conduct any significant military operations. 500,000 tons of iron supplied to Germany by the Soviets in 1939 provided Germany with enough iron reserves to sustain their military for the first 3 ½ years of the second world war. Other forms of metal like manganese were completely absent in Germany, as Germany contains almost no deposits of it. During the re-militarization program prior to World War II, Germany imported 100% of the manganese from the Soviet Union. Manganese was important for the Germans because of its ability to deoxidize steel, which allowed Germany to revamp degraded artillery and restore older machinery, both of which would be traded to the Soviet Union for other minerals. One of the only metals that was ubiquitous in Germany was aluminum, which was normally mixed with other imported minerals to develop logistical equipment like planes. Germany's ability to make full use of resources to maximize economic viability was second to none. Metals and Oil from the Soviet Union allowed Germany to become the advanced military powerhouse it became in the 1930's.

One on hand, it can be pointed out that the Soviet Union aided the German war machine, allowing Germany to subdue much of the western world. On the other hand, one can point out that Germany's export of arms to the Soviet Union during the economic agreement established in the late 1930's provided the Soviet Army with the capability to defeat Germany in World War II.

Other resources which helped foster the German war movement

was food and textiles, which Germany is self-sufficient in producing. Germany was able to domestically produce enough food to keep Germans from starving during the war, and keep soldiers from having to resort to a rationing system. Nevertheless, Germany had looked to import grain from the Soviet Union in order to keep food supply at pre-war levels. The Soviet Union exported 1 million tons of grain to Germany, which maintained Germany's food levels high enough to keep them from rationing. The textiles like cotton exported to Germany from the Soviet Union allowed Germany to maintain the manufacturing of clothing and blankets. By 1941, the Soviets had faithfully honored their part of the agreement, and the Germans were pleased about this. The Soviet Union had been faithful to the detriment for their own needs. Only once in 1940 did the Soviets suspend the economic agreement, but this was because Germany had briefly defaulted on their payments. Germany would resume payments them shortly thereafter.

The manufactured goods that Germany provided to the Soviet Union allowed the Soviets to scale up their arsenal of military equipment. Prior to 1940, Stalin was very aware of how weak the Soviet military was compared to the German one, and the Soviet Union allocated very little of its budget to defense spending between 1936 and 1939. Stalin knew how important it was for the Soviet Union to take steps to mitigate the chances of a German invasion of the country. Hence the reason the Soviets established both an economic and military agreement with the Germans in 1939 and 1940. But despite amassing a powerful military of its own by way of German arms exports to Russia, the Soviet Union would have trouble gaining control over the much smaller nations of Poland and Finland, 2 nations which Russia considered within its sphere of influence. Adhering to the Secret Protocol which called for Germany and Russia to secure their sphere of influence in their respective regions, the Soviet Union invaded both Poland and Finland. The Soviet invasion of eastern Poland took months, compared to the German occupation of Poland which only took them around 3 weeks. This further validated Stalin's outlook of how superior Germany's armed forces were compared to the Soviet's. The lack of efficient communications between Red Army commands in Ukraine and Belarus complicated the Soviet mission to occupy Poland. In 1939, the Soviet military was still a work in progress and much equipment was still lacking. However, Stalin insisted on mobilizing the Red Army for the partition of Poland, but the mission would take a month as weak lines of communication and untrained fighters would stifle the Soviet advance. Nonetheless, the Red Army would continue their offense conquering the Latvia and Estonia before moving into Finland. The Soviet invasion of Finland is strikingly similar to Russia's 2022 invasion of Ukraine in terms of Russia's difficulty in securing and taking control of a much smaller nation with a much smaller military force. Finland was once part of the Russian empire and Russia considered the country to be part of its sphere of influence. Up onto that that time, the Soviet Union had conveyed the desire to bring Finland into the bloc. Initially, the Soviet Union offered to engage Finland diplomatically by requesting that Finland allow them to access their resources and ports. But when the Finnish President refused, Stalin feared that the Finns had already mobilized to fight the Red Army, which led Stalin to launch an all out pre-emptive naval, air force, and ground assault on Finland on November 30 1939. Despite the onslaught by the vastly superior Red Army, which outnumbered the total population of Finland, the Finns were able to resist the Red Army and retain control over their home territory for some time. Stalin believed that he could force the Finnish army to scatter by attacking Finland from multiple sides. However, the Finnish troops were dispersed along the border, which cut off Soviet access to incoming weapons reinforcement, and this kept the Red Army from securing an advantageous position against the Finns. This prolonged the war because the Finns were intially confident they could win, but after a few months, the Finnish command realized that they could not fight forever. After making numerous requests to the allied powers for military aid, the Finns were left alone as the allies refused to bring help. The war reached a stalemate. The Finish resistance eventually broke down amid increasing Red Army troops, and the Red Army would finally take control of the country. In March of 1940, the Finns signed the Moscow Peace Treaty, which provided the Soviet Union access to the Finland's ports and bases in exchange for allowing Finland to retain their sovereignty. After being unable to occupy Poland and Finland in a relatively quick manner, the Soviet military ramped up their defense spending and militarization at frantic speed. In June of 1940, they then set there sights on Romania, in particular Bessarabia and Northern Bukovina. Under the Secret Protocol, the Germans acknowledged Soviet interest in Bessarabia, which came under Soviet occupation after the Soviet Union gave Romania an ultimatum to either evacuate the Romanian military and civil administration from Bessarabia and the northern part of Bukovina, or face a Soviet invasion of the country. Adhering to the advice of German diplomats, the Romanian government would yield to the Soviet demands and cede Bessarabia and northern Bukovina to the Soviet Union. The German Minister of Foreign Affairs, Joachim von Ribbentrop was concerned about how a military conflict would affect the fate of the 100,000 ethnic Germans living in Bessarabia. Ribbentrop also acknowledged that Soviet interest in Bukovina was not part of the Secret Protocol. Hence, it becomes apparent that such overreach by the Soviets, along with Germany's concern about ethnic

Germans living in Bessarabia gave the Germans the justification to break the non-aggression pact with the Soviet Union. Hitler would later state in a conversation with Finland Field Marshall Carl Mannerheim that Germany could not allow the Soviet Union to take the petroleum wells in Romania, noting that without it, there would be no way for the German army to maintain their arsenal of tanks, planes, and various other artillery. Hitler believed that Russia would have attempted to seize all of Romania and annex the petroleum wells, a prospect that would have shattered Germany's war effort. In this conversation, Hitler is also astounded at how the Russian labor forces could amass 35000 tanks at the start of the war. Official estimates on the number of Soviet tanks came to be around 26000. Nevertheless, it was clear that the Soviets salvaged every advantage they could garner from the 1939 economic agreement with Germany. Russia's labor force proved itself extraordinary in quickly making use of the machinery imported from the Germans. The factories that were under construction in the Soviet Union with the help of the Germans in the late 1930s were—within 2 years—as a result of Russia's labor force, mass producing thousands of tanks. Here is the transcript of Hitler conversation with Carl Mannerheim about Russia's military strength and speedy arsenal build-up. This is taken from http://www.feldgrau.ne:

Unidentified (Hitler?): "...a very great danger, perhaps the gravest one..."

Hitler: "(unintelligible)...we ourselves were not completely sure of this, how monstrous this strong armament was."

Mannerheim: "We had not suspected this, in the Winter-War, in the Winter-War we had not suspected this, of course we had a (one unintelligible word) that they were well armed, but so as they had been in fact, and now there is no doubt at all what they had planned ('was sie hatten in ihrem Schild')"

Hitler: "It is evident...evident. They have the most monstrous armament that is humanly conceivable ('menschendenkbar')...so... if anybody had told me that one state...(footsteps)...if anybody had told me that one state can line up with 35.000 tanks (Hitler uses the word 'tank'), I had said 'you have gone mad'...

Unidentified: "Thirty-five..."

Hitler: "35.000 Panzer (now he uses the word 'Panzer')...we have more than, we have at the time more than 34 Pan...thousand Panzer destroyed. If somebody had told me this to...had said: you...if one

general of mine had declared, that a state here had 35.000 tanks, I had said, Mister ('Mein Herr'), you are seeing everything double... or tenfold, this is crazy, you are seeing ghosts...I had not thought this possible...If somebody had told me that...I have told this just before, we have found industrial plants...one of this in (unintelligible: Kalanuskaja?) for example, that was under construction two years ago...and we had no idea...and today there is a tank production facility that...that...in the first shift a bit over 30.000 and in full development should have employed more than 60.000 workers...one single tank production facility...we have occupied it...a gargantuan facility...lots of workers who nevertheless live like animals and such..."

Unidentified: "An amazing region..."

Another Unidentified (Hitler?): "An amazing region..."

Mannerheim: "If one considers that they had for 20 years...more than 20 years...25 years nearly, the freedom to arm themselves... and expended all, all for armament...only armament..."

Hitler: "May I tell you...(couple of unintelligible words)...president of state, I have not suspected this, had I suspected this, my heart would have felt even heavier...but I had made the decision all the more...because there was no other possibility. It was obvious to me, already in winter 39/40 that the (Invasion of the Soviet Union?) had to come. But I had the nightmarish pressure ('Alpdruck') of the West on me, because a war on two fronts, that would have been the downfall...we, too, would have been crushed. We see that better today as we could realize it back then...we would have been crushed...our complete...originally I wanted in autumn 1939 to...I wanted to carry out the West Campaign, only that continuously bad weather we had, that has hindered us. Our whole armament was...it is a 'Good Weather' Armament ('Schönwetterbewaffnung'), it is very capable, it is good, but it is unfortunately a Good Weather Armament. Indeed, we have seen it recently here in this war, naturally all of our weapons are styled ('zugeschnitten') for the west. And we all had the conviction...that was until now (mumbling)...it was just our opinion, since the oldest times...one cannot wage war in wintertime. And we have...the German tanks... the German tanks have not been put to the test to perhaps prepare them for winter-war, but test-runs were made to prove that one cannot wage war in winter. It has been a different starting point. In autumn 1939 we have been facing the question...and I wanted yet to attack under all circumstances...I had the conviction that we would finish France within six weeks...but there was the question wether one would be able to move...and it was this continuously rainy weather...and since I know this French region very well...and I, too, could not discount the opinion of many of my generals, that we, probably, would not achieve this verve ('Elan'), that we would not be able to make full use of the tank force ('Panzerwaffe'), that we would not be able to make full use of the Air Force, too, with the front air fields, because of the rain...I knew northern France myself, I have been soldier for four years during the Great War...and that was the reason for this delay. Had I finished France in the year 39, the world history would have went a different way, but this way I had to wait until the year 1940...and that was not possible until May...the 10th of May was the first fair day, and I have attacked on the 10th of May at once. I have given order on 8th of May to attack on the 10th and...then there had to be...had this giant transposition of our divisions from the west to the east to be made... (unintelligible: the first occupations in...?) then we had this task in Norway...during the same time came...came actually, I can say that today, this very great misfortune upon us, namely the weaknesses that had arisen for Italy, firstly the North-African situation, secondly with the situation in Albania and Greece, a very grave misfortune. We had to help now. That, at a blow, meant for us first of all again a rending of our Air Force, a rending of our tank units... while were preparing our tank units for the east, we had, at a blow, to commit two divisions...two complete divisions, it turned out to be three at the end...and had to replenish very great losses there...it were bloody fights that have been fought out in the desert... naturally all of this has been missing here in the east...and...it was not imaginable any other way that the decision, which has been inevitable. I had a talk back then with Molotov, and it was absolutely obvious...Molotov left with the decision to begin the war, and I dismissed him with the decision to beat him to it, if possible... because, the demands this man was making were obviously aiming at ultimately ruling Europe...(the next sentence is whispered and largely unintelligible, something like 'I have [...] to dispute this, is downright ridiculous [...]')...Already in...in...in autumn 1940 there was constantly this question for us: shall one ...err...risk a sundering?...I have advised the Finnish government back then... err...to negotiate and...err...to gain time to...err...err...to handle things divertoric ('die Sachen divertorisch zu behandeln'- I have to admit that I never encountered the word 'divertorisch' before, but it seems to derive from the latin 'divertere' – to deflect, akin to the English 'divert'), because I always had one fear: that Russia would suddenly assault Romania in late autumn, and would annex the petroleum sources...and we would have been not finished yet in late autumn 1940. If Russia had occupied the Romanian petroleum sources, Germany would have been lost...(unintelligible one or two

words, something with 'need'?)...with...with, with 60 Russian divisions this thing could have been arranged; back then we had in Romania no task force yet, the Romanian government has turned to us very lately...and what we had would have been ridiculous indeed. They only would have needed to occupy the petroleum sources, I could not have started a war in September or October any more with our arms, that was indeed impossible...we also had the deployment of our troops in the east not prepared in any way, the units had to be consolidated in the west first, the armament had to be brought in order...because, naturally, we had also have made our sacrifices during the West Campaign. It would have been impossible to line up before the Spring of 1941, and if now the Russian, back then in the autumn of 1940, had occupied Rumania, and had annexed the petroleum sources, then we would have been... err...helpless in the year 1941...We had...have the large German production, but the amount the Air Force alone is consuming, the amount our tank-divisions are consuming that is something quite monstrous. It is a...a...a consumption surpassing all imagination. And without the afflux of four to five million tons of Rumanian petroleum, we would not be able to wage the war.... (Unintelligible, a few words, some of them 'had to let'?)...And this worried me greatly, hence my attempt to overcome this time through negotiations, until we were strong enough to oppose this extortionate demands...the demands were sheer extortion, it were extortions, the Russians knew that we were helpless, that we were tied in the west, they could extort everything from us...and only on the visit of Molotov...then I have offhandedly declared them, that we could not accept the demands...these many demands...Basically with this the negotiations were...abruptly ended...(a few unintelligible words)...there were four points, the one point concerning Finland...was the freedom to protect themselves from the Finnish threat...I said: 'You do not want to tell me that Finland is threatening you?...He said, well, in Finland one would act against the friends of the Soviet Union...this would be a society... they would be continuously persecuted, and a Great Power could not accept being threatened from a small state regarding its existence.' I said: ' you...your existence is not threatened by Finland, is it? You are not trying to tell me that your existence is threatened by Finland?' (In the background someone says: 'ridiculous.') Well, there also would be a moral threat to the existence of a Great State, and what Finland was doing would be the mor...a threat to the moral existence...And I said to him, that we would not be able to accept another war on the Baltic Sea as passive spectators. Then he asked me how our positions would be regarding Romania, we had made a guarantee after all...whether this guarantee would be directed against Russia as well...I said: 'I

do not think that it is directed against you, because you do not have the intention to assault Romania, don't you? Tell me...we never have heard that you have the intention to assault Romania, you have always stated that Bessarabia belonged to you, but you have never stated that you wanted to assault Romania.' He said that he wanted to know precisely..."

(End of Audio-Recording)

To this day, dependence on foreign oil has been mainstay for the German economy. Perhaps only a revolting prospect should Germany attempt to displace itself from the security umbrella of the North Atlantic Treaty Organization (NATO), and attempt to reassert its pre-1945 geopolitical independence. As a member of NATO, Germany has had the luxury of spending less of its budget for military purposes, which lent Germany the status of being the number four economy in the world, superseded only by Japan, China, and the United States. After Germany was defeated in World War II, the country was occupied by Soviet and US forces. Some ideas about what should happen to Germany immediately begin to be discussed. It was proposed that Germany be broken up into smaller states to prevent it from threatening its neighbors again. Other believed it would be more beneficial to have Germany maintain a strong economy, all while being incorporated into a united Europe. Germany had only been a sovereign nation state since 1871, largely due in part to Prussia's military strength. Also, the United States proposed dividing Germany into 3 sectors, all geared to agriculture, as opposed to heavy industry. This plan was offered by US Secretary of the Treasury, Henry Morgenthau in 1944. President Herbert Hoover, however, was more concerned about the humanitarian implications of jeopardizing Germany's ability to feed its citizens as well as incoming refugees coming from the east. Much of Hoover's fear stemmed from the way hunger gave way to the Bolshevik revolution during and after the first world war. Hoover did not want a repeat of such a scenario post World War II, and he also believed that starving the Germans would only compel them to drift into the Soviet Union's sphere of influence and take up communist ideologies. Moreover, the main component that the allies wanted to eliminate from Germany was militarism and Nazism. Prior to World War II, Germany's economy could be regarded as a form of organized capitalism where big corporations would be led by large board members who would collude for the purposes of increasing profits and stifling any incoming competition. Germany was known for protecting its big businesses, such as arms manufacturer, Krupp and chemicals company, I.G. Farben, both of whom profited substantially from the Nazi arms industry. The allies

considered this consortium aspect in Germany's economy to operate much like a cartel. Hence, why the allies were adamant about breaking up this amalgamation of private economic power, as well as demilitarizing Germany. The allies believed that the arms movement in Germany was largely maintained and supported by the influence of a wealthy consortium of private business owners. Furthermore, it was not just demilitarizing and decartelizing that the allies set out to achieve for Germany, the central core intent was de-nazification of the country. This denazification intended to remove all Nazis and sympathizers from all aspects of German life, including politics and government. *(We see Russian President Vladimir Putin take a page from this post World War II scenario to justify his invasion of Ukraine in 2022, which he described as the attempt to denazify the country's government.)* It was also agreed upon by the allies that Germany must pay reparations, namely to France and the Soviet Union.

Chapter 6: Germany's Economic Miracle

In 1945, the Allies began the process of deciding how Germany would be divided. The US occupation zone was in the south. The British occupation zone was in the west and the north. The French occupation zone was in the south and west. And the Soviet occupation zone was in central part of Germany. The eastern part was controlled by Poland, where the Soviets had that same year installed a pro-Soviet government. So technically the eastern and central part of Germany would come under communist influence. This division of Germany into 4 zones was confirmed at the 1945 Potsdam conference. Also, those territories that were annexed and conquered by the Nazis before and during World War II were effectively reassigned back to those nations that originally ceded the territory to the Germans. Germany under Adolf Hitler invaded and annexed Austria, Czechoslovakia, Belgium, France, Italy, Luxembourg, Poland and Yugoslavia. The allies approved of detaching German lands east of the Oder–Neisse line, and placing them under the control of the Polish and Soviet administrations. This was done to compensate the Polish for some of the eastern portions of Poland that were lost to the Soviet Union when the Soviet Union annexed eastern Poland in 1939. Those eastern territories east of the Oder–Neisse line would no longer be recognized as Allied-occupied territory. The remainder of defeated Germany would be governed jointly by US, British, French, and Soviet forces. Berlin, in and of itself, would undergo the same 4-way split among the allied powers. Despite these cooperative efforts, the divergent economic policies pursued for US, British, and French controlled territories and for Soviet controlled territories would ultimately split Germany into 2 states—East and West Germany and initiate the Cold War. The French, British, and US controlled areas were seeking to establish a framework of private business and democratically established governance. The Soviet zone, on the other hand, was looking to establish single party rule and state controlled industry. This inability to find common ground reached a tipping point when the French, British, and US controlled areas, which had become known as the tri-zone, decided on June 19, 1948 to issue a new currency called the Deutsche Mark(West German Mark) to replace the Reichmark, which was still being used throughout all of Germany. The Deutsche Mark, however, had quickly circulated throughout Berlin and became the standard currency there. The Soviet zone responded in kind by issuing, shortly thereafter on June 23, 1948, what was called the East German Mark. The very next day, the Soviets blocked West Germany's access to Berlin, refusing to lift the blockade until the non-Soviet zones agreed to accept the East German mark as legal tender for all of Germany. Access to Berlin via

rail, road and water was cut off until May of 1949. The western sectors, however, got around the blockade by using aircraft to bring in supplies to their respective zones in Berlin. The fiasco led to the formal creation of 2 independent states in Germany.

The formulation of a constitution for the West German state began in 1948 when the western allies committed to giving governing authority back to the Germans. In July of 1948, the western allies issued the Frankfurt documents, which called for a layout of parameters for developing the constitution, which was expected to be drafted by the Germans themselves. The framework was to involve a strong democracy that left room for centralized authority and basic rights. It was made clear that this formulation did not entail West Germany's complete sovereignty from allied control, especially in terms of foreign policy, trade, and national emergencies. The parameters attempted to appeal to the basic tenets of most political entities in West Germany at the time, namely the Social Democrats and the Christian Democrats. The Social Democrats desired a more centralized state, while the Christian democrats insisted on maintaining influence on cultural and school issues. Much of West Germany firmly believed that Church should be integrated with State, while individuals be granted the freedom to choose their faith. This move to develop an official West German state affirmed the reality of Germany becoming split, but this did not concern West German citizens since this constitution was termed "Basic Law", which thus gave it a temporary notion. This "Basic Law" was developed in 2 phases. The first phase was when officials from the 11 state (Lander) governments called a meeting at the old Herrenchiemsee castle in Bavaria to discuss and develop a draft constitution, establish the legal framework, and draw the lines between what comprised state jurisdiction and what comprised federal jurisdiction. The second phase was the development of a Parliamentary Council, whose members were appointed by the state governments. The Parliamentary Council consisted of representatives from the major political parties, all appointed by the state governments and vetted by the allies after a rigorous denazification screening. The Council consisted of 70 delegates; 5 of which were non-voting, and they were tasked with developing West Germany's new "Basic Law." On May 23, 1949, the Parliamentary Council formally announced the formation of the Federal Republic of Germany(FRG) with the city of Bonn designated as the provisional capital. This new republic was guided by a legislative assembly called the Bundestag, meant to serve as the most powerful constitutional body intended to operate within the parameters of what the "Basic Law" defined as basic rights and basic principles of human dignity. To enforce this requirement, the Parliamentary Council established the Constitutional Court, which would review grievances that

German citizens had with the state. Under the "Basic Law", the powers of the president were limited and facilitated from the Bundestag. Many on the right considered this limitation of the powers of the president as a reinforcement that Germany was disqualified from tending to their own security as it related to domestic and foreign affairs. Some even railed against the idea of a system that forfeits the power of the executive and awards it to the political parties.

The Federal Republic held their first elections on August 14, 1949, with nearly 15 political parties participating in the event. The Christian Democrats and the Free Democrats forged an alliance and would come out victorious, as Konrad Adenauer would be elected Chancellor, and Theodor Heuss of the Free Democratic Party would become West Germany's first president. Together, with the economics minister, Ludwig Erhard, all three would set Germany on the course of economic recovery by following a social market economic strategy. Business was left in the hands of the private sector, while the market would be allowed to decide prices and wages. Just prior to the formation of the Federal Republic of Germany, the new currency, the Deutschmark(West German Mark), issued by the tri-zone caused unemployment to rise since the Deutschmark initially raised the cost of labor, causing employers to cut their workforce and wages for the sake of keeping expenses minimized. However, with Marshal Aid provided to Germany by the US, the Deutschmark was strengthened and legitimized, which opened the door to foreign investment. Another factor that cultivated this economic miracle was the fact that profits were increasing as wages continued to remain low. At this time, many of the incoming refugees moving to West Germany from East Germany were both educated and highly skilled, and this influx had kept the demand for work higher than the supply of jobs. This is attributed to the fact that much of the communist elements in West Germany were suppressed, and those who propagated Marxism were shunned, both from work and society as a whole, which kept workplace militancy to a minimum. Also, labor unions which were crushed by the Nazis remained subdued even after World War II under reconstruction. Another .element is that at this time in Germany, it was easy for businesses to exploit exiles, who were also highly skilled and educated. All things considered, a cheap but highly skilled and educated workforce is likely the main catalyst that triggered West Germany's economic miracle. As the West German economy continued to expand in the 1950s, demand would follow. Germans, after having gone through a war and the destruction of their country, were eager to consume and acquire goods that they hadn't enjoyed since before the war. Things from furniture to clothes to cars to TV sets were all consumed by the West German public, whose standard of living had begun to increase substantially. Some of the factors that may have kept the economy from expanding further was the denazification efforts which would oftentimes remove top technical expertise from the workforce.

It was discovered that the economic boom of the 1950s produced a side-effect of neglecting the elderly and disabled. Throughout the timeframe of the first Federal Republic government, pension issues and life insurance policies were largely ignored, owing to the fact that the war had gobbled up much of the private pension and life insurance funds. The policy that the FRG had set up for pensions was very ineffective, and the Christian Democrats did not have the urgency to apply reforms. As a consequence, the Social Democrats would look to seize the example of the government's lack of action on pension reform and use that to their advantage at the polls. The move prompted Adenauer to push a pension reform bill through legislation in 1957, which provided retirees, unemployed, and disabled with 60% of their average annual income which would be adjusted to currency wage levels, all for the sake of ensuring that the standard of living for retirees, disabled, and unemployed would not fall below the rest of the population in West Germany. As a result of this action by Adenauer, the Christian Democrats would win the 1957 election. And by the end of the 1950's, West Germany would turn into a social welfare state as a result of this amalgamation of free market policies with social democratic values.

East Germany would quickly respond to the formation of the Federal Republic of Germany by establishing the German Democratic Republic(GDR). Much like West Germany establishing the Federal Republic of Germany to serve and lean in the direction of the economic backdrop of the west and its free-market values, East Germany established the German Democratic Republic to integrate eastern economic communist systems. The Soviet economic system was antithetical to the western system in that the Soviet communist system relied on command rather than market direction. Thus the Soviet occupiers of East German territories would remove anti-communist elements and people from power and replace them with pro-Soviet, pro-communist Germans. The state would become dominated by one party, the Socialist Unity Party, made up of German communists who would look to emulate the governing structure of the Soviet Union. The GDR nationalized banks and major corporations, as well as land reform....all intended to stifle the formation of economic class division. The communists in East Germany would often justify the implementation of communism in Germany by pointing out how Communism's very founders, Karl Marx and Frederick Engels, were both German. Many of the German communists had been exiled by the Nazi Party during Hitler's reign, and quite a number of them were sent to concentration camps. After

World War II, they returned to East Germany to assist in the rebuilding process. Many of them had no experience in public administration or municipal planning, nor any knowledge on how to go about wielding power. The German communists were motivated by an idealism of what Germany should become, and within this hope, they had no concrete blueprint on how this ideal was to come to fruition. Much of their actions were predicated on moves by the west. Even still, most Germans had no ambitions to establish a separate state. When the German Democratic Republic was announced, along with the proclamation of building it as a socialist state, a number of detractors predicted that the attempt would prove futile and that the GDR would only last a few months before collapsing. Numerous attempts were made to sabotage the newly established republic. Throughout its existence, the GDR was marred by endless attempts to undermine its economy and legislative procedures. West Germany's economic recovery was constantly promoted to reinforce the inferiority of the GDR's attempt at socialism. The increasing number of Germans fleeing East Germany for West Germany for better salaries stifled the aims of the GDR, and many East Germans used the availability of employment in West Germany to leverage demands that they receive higher salaries in East Germany. This is the reason why the Berlin Wall was built in 1961—to deter emigration of East Germans to West Germany. Another factor that allowed the FRG to undermine GDR's economic growth was due to both West Germany's economic expansion and the fact that East Germans migrating there were automatically regarded as citizens of the FRG. They would be provided all the necessary paperwork and an easy path to securing a house and job. Many of these migrants from the GDR to the FRG were white collar workers—doctors, dentists, and engineers. Thus, the outflow of skilled labor from the GDR curtailed its ability to foster economic growth. During the first 20 years of the GDR's existence, it had increasing difficulty in establishing and sustaining diplomatic ties with countries outside of the communist sphere, and this was because West Germany placed a lot of pressure on nations that were looking to recognize the GDR or establish diplomatic relations with them. The FRG's stance maintained a refusal to continue relations with nations that would try and establish ties with the GDR. However, Egypt, which was receiving aid from the Federal Republic of Germany, became the first non-communist country to recognize the German Democratic Republic. This was certainly to the dismay of the FRG, and when the GDR Prime Minister planned to visit Egypt after the recognition, a number of western nations closed their airspace and prohibited the flight from traveling to Egypt over their territory. As a consequence, the Prime Minister was forced to get there via Yugoslavia or boat. This is an example of how pettiness could arise during the Cold War. Such tensions made it increasingly difficult for the GDR to maintain its trading links with West German firms, who were under heightened pressure to sever ties with the socialist/communist state. The GDR was economically reliant on these trading relationships, and the abrupt termination of contracts suppressed the GDR's ability to recover from World War II. Isolating East Germany is different than isolating Eastern Europe, in that Germany itself is reliant on imports for raw materials, where eastern European countries like Russia sits on a vast variety of raw materials, allowing them to be less dependent of acquiring minerals from elsewhere. Without adequate supply chain of raw materials, East Germany's attempt to establish its manufacturing industry was largely deficient. Further difficulty the GDR encountered came about when in 1951, the FRG imposed a steel embargo and banned trade between West Germany and East Germany. This would prove to be devastating since one of the main materials that Germany was abundant in was blocked from reaching East Germany. That material was coal.

East Germany had since the beginning of the post-war era made numerous efforts to retain some semblance of peace and harmony and coexistence. Even after the GDR was created, Stalin would request that a treaty with the Federal Republic be formulated—an effort that was rejected by FRG Chancellor Adenauer since the FRG refused to recognize the GDR. Once it became obvious that the United States was going to remilitarize West Germany and incorporate them into NATO, the dynamics of the relationship between east and west would take on considerable change. In 1955, the FRG established the Bundeswehr, which was to serve as West Germany's official armed forces. East Germany, in 1956, established the Volksarmee to be the official armed forces of East Germany. At this juncture, Stalin's policy of peaceful accordance between East and West Germany was off the table.

The GDR is credited with being able to maintain a more egalitarian society devoid of the class privilege that had been a staple in pre-war Germany where the top sectors of society had been dominated by the wealthier citizenry. In pre-war Germany, women were largely confined to domestic and low-salary employment. The GDR looked to change this since when it comes to gender equality, communism has been the best of the best ideologies. The GDR took steps to counter class and gender division by ensuring an equal pay system, in which higher level positions were not granted significantly more pay than lower level positions. This aspect of communism comes under criticism from free-market advocates who believe that such an arrangement deters innovation and effort since the result or reward takes less into account than western capitalism —education, skill, and output. Nevertheless, the GDR continued to push this form of equality, leading to East Germany becoming the most egalitarian society in Europe at the time. Even the housing situation in terms of architectural quality accommodated a mix of working class people, with little difference in the standard of living between lower tier employees and upper tier workers. This helped mitigate the possibility of evoking the class tension that typically arises in western societies. Still and all, the social market economy and the higher salaries of West Germany would often lure away top talent from the GDR. For the mainstream sector of society, however, a certain confidence would permeate, a confidence in the sense of security offered by the economic structure of the German Democratic Republic. It was such that fear of things like unemployment, homelessness, lack of access to healthcare and social service were largely absent, and it had become nearly impossible for a person living in East Germany to fall elusive to the social safety net. Employment and housing was guaranteed, and so was healthcare and other services. The catch 22 to removing the fear arising from the potential of experiencing various forms of destitution was that people had more time to dedicate their energies towards social and mental pursuits, which would at times disconcert the state. But overall, there was a sense of duty for the more gifted to pick up the slack left by the less gifted, and at the same time allow the entire entity, whatever it may be—the class, the work environment, the group—to revel in the achievement. In contrast to the western capitalistic outlook, the socialistic perspective in east Germany was less about the individual and more about the good of society. As a result, social integration was much more embedded into the society of east Germany and its soviet-style communism. There was no gender discrimination, people did not feel as though they needed to compete with each other. The old was not set against the young. This was much unlike capitalist countries, where demographics that display a comparative advantage in a certain endeavor can be exploited to the detriment of society's sense of fairness.

Another positive aspect of GDR communism was that communities were much safer since poverty and isolation was quelled by the fact that most people felt a sense of responsibility for happened in their environment. Hence, why people living in the GDR had little to fear in terms of their own communities. People were able to stay outside during late hours without fear of being harassed or victimized. And if these things did occur, they would be very rare incidents. Also, advertising in the GDR didn't involve the exploitation of women, and children were the responsibility of the entire community, not just the single family. I was common for neighbors to take a concerted interest in the welfare of the child, and because of this, things like mental illness and antisocial behavior became less prevalent as most children in that type of society felt cared for. The architectural structure of residential areas in Germany, both east and west, were made up of blocks of flats, but in the GDR, these flats would be owned by the entire community or co-ops, and the residents that lived in those flats consisted of a diverse variety of workers from handymen to teachers to train operators to academic professors, all living next to one another. Thus one's living situation was not a determinant to one's value to society. The responsibility for maintaining the residential spaces and the surrounding public areas fell upon everyone's shoulders, and residents would often take turns carrying out various tasks from lawn-care to snow removal, and the compensation received would be held in a common fund that was supplemented with money received from recycling, a popular practice in the GDR. And much of this was not just for the sake of the environment; it was also largely due in part to the fact that raw materials were scarce in Germany, and people needed to conserve whatever they could get their hands on. Furthermore, this practice did accommodate the later climate change movement by expanding to help promote urgency about global warming and the need to engage in environmentally friendly practices. In the GDR, recycling was very simple, as one could go to a recycling station and exchange items for compensation, which oftentimes motivated more people to take up recycling. Residential organizations would also get involved in the recycling movement and use the money built up in the common fund to enhance the residential community by constructing spaces for various pursuits like hobbies, storage, or parties. In some cases, residential organizations would pay out a percentage of the common fund holdings to each tenant.

Women's rights were outlined in the GDR constitution drafted in 1949, and was geared towards preventing marriage from undermining the rights of women to assist society at the local and national level. The Gesetz über die Rechte der Frau Law guaranteed financial assistance for mothers and made it illegal for employers to terminate a woman's employment due to pregnancy. The law also granted both single and married mothers the same civil rights, and mandated the construction of facilities for children, faculties such as kindergartens and nurseries. These accommodations allowed women to pursue various occupations and at the same time achieve financial independence. That being so, women in the GDR projected a more confident image compared to women of the west. In the GDR, the husband trying to impede the career ambitions of his wife were grounds for divorce, unlike in the FRG where men were the sole owners of property and married women were only allowed to work if they were granted permission by their husbands. In the GDR, women with children could work full-time. In the FRG, they could only work par-time at most. The GDR had programs in place that were specifically geared for the advancement of women. In fact, most of the modern feminist demands in western societies were already embedded in the communist framework. In the GDR, abortion was legal and birth control was ubiquitous. Maternity leave was generous, paying 90% of the woman's salary, and as soon as the baby was born, the family would be awarded 1000 marks.

Socialism in the GDR also lived up to its billing as the prototypical system that centered around the rights of workers. In fact, the rights of workers in the GDR were a top the list of priorities for the socialist state since the Communist Manifesto, written by Marx and Engles, was based on worker liberation from the exploitative capitalist system. Under Communism, the proletariat was to be the pillar of society, and work itself was upheld as the highest honor, regardless of what one's vocation was, whether it be a lower paying job or higher paying job. All of it was considered as a necessity to the sustained functionality of society. Thus, in the GDR, the workers were regarded as the driver of society since it was they who produced the goods and services that the society required. Under communism in the GDR, workers in mines and steel mills who put their health and safety on the line were compensated with better salaries and healthcare than white collar workers who engaged in less hazardous work. Work became a person's birthright under the GDR; even those with criminal backgrounds could secure employment in the socialist system. It was all-inclusive, and employers were tasked to train everyone and give everyone a sense of self-worth, even the disabled. The job security that socialism guaranteed made the workplace more relaxing and managers less authoritarian. This is was in contrast to many places of employment in western societies where the threat of termination or verbal abuse is used to drive output. In the GDR, however, one had to engage in serious delinquency in order lose their job. This delinquency included behavior that was intended to oppose the state, which was also taken very seriously, and the reprisal would often be termination or demotion. Moreover, when it came to voicing grievances in the workplace, employees garnered a significant advantage since in doing so, they would not risk losing their jobs. Thus, employees could point out things they felt needed to be changed at work without serious cost. This fostered an environment that was open to change and improvement and job satisfaction. Strikes did occur sometimes, especially when changes applied upset the workforce. But these were not often and every effort was made to keep worker sentiment from reaching that point. It was also the case that when someone was fired from their job, they would almost immediately be offered alternative employment. The drawback of this system is that it was not in itself a proponent of idleness.

Everyone who could, had to work, and the GDR had no system of offering unemployment benefits. Work was central to life and workers were involved in the company's core issues. Trade Unions were established under the supervision of the state and ensured the continued well-being of the workforce by way of social service availability. Employers, by law, were responsible for ensuring that their employees had access to the basic social safety net programs such as childcare, healthcare, housing, and other accommodations. Many places of employment had medical facilities on site, making it easier for ill workers to access medical attention in a timely manner, lowering the mortality risk that arises from late diagnoses of terminal illnesses. Even though housing was in short supply in the GDR, employers were instrumental in helping employees obtain housing, and major companies were often allocated multiple housing units to provide to their employees in need of residential services. Some places of employment were also equipped with childcare accommodations such as kindergarten and nurseries, provided to help those employees who had children. The workplace also provided meals and recreational facilitates to their workers.

Due to the fact that the GDR did not have the financial backing that West Germany had with the Marshall Plan, their only option for development became the implementation of a command economy backed by centralized state supervision. This is what socialism offered, and the state's five year plans for the economy helped initiate the GDR's heavy industry sector. Shipyards, gas and iron production plants, a new oil refinery were a testament to the GDR's version of economic progress. While not on the level of economic growth as the FRG, the GDR nonetheless achieved self-sufficiency and had one of the most successful economies among socialist countries. Industries that revolved around machinery employed a million people in East Germany, and these industries comprised of highly skilled engineering sectors, and much like pre-war Germany, the GDR had become a top industrial nation and a major exporter of high-level machinery to eastern European countries. Much of the GDR's relative success to other eastern bloc nations is credited to public ownership of industry and the state's central planning process. Over 90% of the assets in the GDR were publicly owned. Yet even as a socialist society, the state managed to make room for private ownership in which the state would have a stake in the company. A private sector did exist in the GDR, but it was relatively small. However, in terms of how much it contributed to the GDP, it was quite significant as the 176,800 private entrepreneurs in the GDR produced an output that made up 2.8% of the GDP. The private sector was made up of artists, writers, craftsmen, retailers, and farmers.

Profits garnered by publicly owned companies were distributed based on the needs of the society, and a large portion was reinvested back into the economy. In the 1960's some of those aforementioned private individual enterprises would join with the publicly owned sectors in what was called VVBs. Together, they would work on research and development for the sake of advancing the sector as a whole. In this regard, the central planning aspect of socialism would try to adopt and integrate some aspects of privatization in way that benefited the society without undermining the socialist structure. Much like the command economy in the Soviet Union, the state would set the production goals, but the VVB would determine the amount of financing the company would need. If the goals were met, bonuses would be distributed, and such prospects would help incentivize workers to become more efficient.

The GDR leadership faced a conundrum in implementing its economic policy. In order to ensure the satisfaction of the proletariat by ensuring the availability of goods and service and offering social programs that compensate for other factors that could impede productivity, the GDR found that the level of productivity in the GDR was not enough to pay for those goods and services. This left the GDR having to rely financially on the FRG, leading to increased borrowing and less reinvestment at home. The GDR was hoping that advancing technology would solve this conundrum, which is why they poured large sums of resources into innovation groups. The state's expenses did not equal it's production, and many of the economic experts in the government of the GDR became concerned about a debt crisis coming about from an increased reliance on the west. But the Socialist Unity Party, however, disregarded this concern, even in light of the fact that none of the countries in the western world would accept the GDR's currency, the East German mark, in return for their products. Much of the west wanted hard currency. This left the GDR having to try and find hard currency in order to meet this demand. So in 1971, after the Ospolitik agreement via the FRG and GDR's signing of the Moscow Treaty which ruled out the use of military force between East and West Germany, the GDR began encouraging westerners to travel to the East Germany, but the catch was that they would purchase East German marks at a 1:1 ratio, meaning that 1 East German Mark would be equal to one unit of hard western currency. This was set up in order to generate more income for the state and in a way, let westerners subsidize the GDR. Visitors would come to the GDR to visit family and would often times come bearing gifts, one of which would be hard currency from the west. Being aware of this factor, the GDR would open up shops selling popular western merchandise at higher prices. They also expanded their level of credit with the FRG, and would leverage the release of political prisoners for western loans. The GDR and FRG began negotiating directly with each other on the sale of goods. All of these thing likely deterred the GDR's impending financial collapse. The cost to the GDR was that it would go into deep debt to West Germany, a country it long considered its main nemesis. The lack of raw materials as well would impact the East German economy. Not to mention the housing issue. In the GDR, only 5% of the worker income was relegated to rents, which left no surplus that the housing association could invest into property repairs and improvements. The GDR deciding to defer such expenses led to numerous buildings depreciating in value and structure. The continued operation of coal plants led to environmental issues such as air and water pollution. And updated equipment was unable to be acquired, leaving workers having to rely on outdated equipment and spend a good deal of time repairing them, which cut into productivity and the quality of goods. Also living standards for the elderly population in the GDR dwindled. All things considered, much of Germany's historical deficiencies in raw materials had come to back to stifle the GDR's efforts at self-sufficiency, a long-standing but elusive goal of the German state. The growing debt accumulation by the GDR to the west restricted the policy goals of East Germany. The increased economic reliance on the FRG hindered the ability of the GDR to crush dissent within their own territories since human rights violations could lead to the FRG cutting their financial aid to the country. Thus the GDR would no longer push a policy of shooting people that were trying emigrate to West Germany.

Tension between the Soviet Union and the GDR began to grow as the Soviet Union began finding new customers for their oil exports. After the 1973 oil embargo in which OPEC refused to sell oil to nations supporting Israel during the Yom Kippur War, the Soviet Union was afforded the opportunity to develop a lucrative energy trade with the west. Experiencing financial problems of their own, the Soviet Union began cutting their oil exports to the GDR, and increasing them to the FRG. And this was likely due to the low quality of goods being produced by the GDR for those previously mentioned reasons like workers being stuck with outdated equipment and having to spend more time repairing them as opposed to producing quality goods. This reduction of energy exports from the Soviet Union had negative systemic implications for the GDR, and GDR officials expressed their fear to the Soviet Union that less oil would undermine the GDR economy and destabilize their country. But nevertheless, the Soviet Union remained adamant about reducing oil exports to the GDR, which led to heightened tensions and further reductions and the fact that those factors would lead the GDR into having to rely more heavily on financial aid from the west. This was another conundrum. Even though the Soviet Union was developing its oil trade with the west, they still insisted that East Germany limit its correspondence with the FRG. When Erich Honecker, General Secretary of the Socialist Unity Party of Germany, planned to attend a summit with the Chancellor of the FRG, the Soviet Union forbade the meeting. In this regard, the GDR for the sake of its economy was forced to rely more on the west because the Soviet Union decided to limit its exports to the GDR, but at the same time the Soviet Union would attempt to discourage the GDR from further developing its relations with the FRG. The United States was still on the Soviet Union's radar as a result of the ongoing Cold War. When the North Atlantic Treaty Organization(NATO) expanded its western military bloc to include West Germany in 1955, the Soviet Union followed a similar course by establishing its own eastern military bloc called the Warsaw Pact and integrated East Germany into the alliance.

Tensions between the Soviet Union and East Germany would ease temporarily when Mikhail Gorbachev became its General Secretary in 1985. At the outset, Mikhail Gorbachev sought to establish western-friendly reforms in the Soviet Union, even adopting some free-market principles in an attempt to revive the Soviet Union's declining economy. He also considered East German communism to be the example for the economies of eastern Europe. Despite the financial problems taking place in the GDR, Gorbachev noted how much more efficient it was than other socialist countries in eastern Europe. However, within a short time, the Soviet Union under Gorbachev would cut deliveries of oil and raw materials to East Germany, and the GDR would respond by becoming contrarian to Gorbachev's reforms. One such reform of Gorbachev was glasnost, which essentially gave citizens in the Soviet Union the right to exercise free speech. The GDR feared that this would spread to East Germany, and in 1988 the government there doubled down on suppressing free speech. They also banned the Soviet journal, Sputnik, from East Germany. These measures were met with hostility from not only the public, but also from members within the Socialist Unity Party who long considered the Soviet Union as the basis for its existence and also the model that East Germany was to emulate. General Secretary of the Socialist Unity Party, Erich Honecker, had come to power on a pro-Soviet platform, so neither the public nor his constituents understood his sudden anti-Sovet outlook. Much of East Germany had bought into Gorbachev's willingness to invite change, but the same could not be said for Honecker. Honecker was also concerned about Gorbachev's move to assert "freedom of choice" for the Soviet Union's client states, which implied a hands-off approach, a revolting prospect for nation states such as the GDR that were reliant on the Soviet Union militarily. Even so, some in the Socialist Unity Party welcomed this idea of policy freedom because it would give them more flexibility. Another

dilemma would arise. Since the fact of being militarily dependent on the Soviet Union made it easy for the GDR to adhere to a standard that only reinforced its communist paradigm, the notion of non-intervention pushed by Gorbachev only served to bring the GDR further into the sphere of western influence since it was the case that the GDR was financially reliant on the FRG and the west. Many in the Socialist Unity Party began discourse about the possibility of a united Germany. And of course, Honecker was certainly alarmed at this prospect. Unsurprisingly as a result of Gorbachev's lenient doctrine for eastern Europe, dissent that had formed all throughout East Germany during the decade of the 80s and were now being practiced by an increasing number of regular citizens, set the stage for the 1989 East German Revolution. Throughout the 80s, millions of petitions were sent to the GDR by regular citizens who were demanding the right to leave the country, and in 1989, the GDR would pass a new emigration law that would adhere to the Helsinki accords—a contract established in 1975 between the Soviet bloc and western nations to agree on human rights and basic freedoms—and at the same time reduce emigration from East Germany. Despite the effort, thousands of East German citizens applied to vacate the GDR. Gorbachev doing away with the Brezhnev Doctrine, which affirmed Soviet intervention in eastern European states, gave way to independence movements throughout eastern Europe. Under Gorbachev, countries in the Soviet bloc were allowed to vote for other parties besides the communists during elections. Such became the case in Hungary, who would shift from communist rule to a multi-party democracy, allowing them to break the barriers established between them and neighboring Austria. The result was that Hungary would seek closer ties with the west. This allowed citizens of East Germany to use Hungary as a means to escape to West Germany. They would simply travel to Hungary, then to Austria and make their way into West Germany from there. Hungary, nevertheless, adhered to their agreement with the GDR to extradite emigrants back to East Germany. However, West German Chancellor Kohl would intervene and release East German emigrants being detained at the West German embassy in Budapest, Hungary, and allow them entry into West Germany. This had a ripple effect, as many more East German citizens would attempt to make their way to West German embassies in Poland and Czechoslovakia and seek asylum. Looking to save face, the GDR General Secretary Honecker made a deal to permit the emigration of those seeking refuge at West German embassies if the east German citizens would return to East Germany and be formally expelled. This had little effect as mass emigration began taking place in East Germany, leading to the GDR cutting off free transport to Prague, Czechoslovakia in order to stop it.

The GDR refused to adhere to Gorbachev's voting reforms, and in 1989, the local elections throughout the country still consisted of one party, the Socialist Unity Party, with citizens only being able to vote for a unity candidate. The Soviet Union, Poland, and Hungary had already applied reforms to their voting policy. Furthermore, many local organizations were getting concerned about a violent revolution as the GDR secret police continued taking action against a growing dissident movement. Nevertheless the dissident movement continued to grow and number of them would establish various independence groups. A domino effect ensued, and officials began walking away from the Socialist Unity Party as it was clear that without Soviet intervention, the GDR was not equipped to quell a dissident movement of hundreds of thousands of people. After Honecker was removed from power, the Socialist Unity party made a last ditch effort to try and honor demands for a new travel regulation, and at the same time deter mass exodus of GDR citizens from East Germany. Attempts to dialogue with the new autonomous social organizations only further diminished the credibility of the party in asserting its singularity in East Germany's affairs. The other problem was the GDR's longstanding debts to the west which had been accrued over a 20 year period, a problem that GDR refused to resolve with spending cuts. The major flash-point for the dissident movement had been travel regulation, and when the GDR had decided to address the issue by introducing a new travel regulation effective immediately on November 9, 1989, one that would allow—according to the GDR press spokesperson's statement—for GDR citizens to leave the German Democratic Republic through any border crossing, citizens in East Berlin began gathering near multiple checkpoints. Despite no formal plans to open the border, guards at the checkpoints lifted the traffic barriers and the people flooded thru. The fall of the Berlin Wall set in motion the reunification of East and West Germany.

It had been clear that much of the factors that have economically plagued Germany for decades repeated themselves during the time of the Soviet-backed East German state—The German Democratic Republic. While the GDR had one of the most efficient implementations of socialism in eastern Europe, the lack of raw materials there and the constant emigration of technical expertise to West Germany had ultimately placed an expiration date on the governing body. At the same time, one can look at the example of both pre-war and post war Germany and see that Germany's number one commodity was it own ethnic German demographic. Exportation of German scientists and engineers to Russia, to West Germany, and to the United States played a central role in the technological advancement of those nations.

After the fall of the Berlin Wall, discourse about how East and

West Germany should go about re-unification became a major talking point. There were some concerns, however. The United States for instance was somewhat worried about how a re-unified Germany would evaluate its place in NATO since was formed mainly in part to stifle Germany's future military ambitions. Others felt that after the horrors perpetrated by Germany during World War II, Germany itself did not deserve to re-unite. Meanwhile, the FRG would keep an eye over the situation, still aware that East and West Germany had been ideologically divergent for quite some time. Nonetheless, the FRG Chancellor Kohl continued to help facilitate East German migration into West Germany, just as he would continue to assert West Germany's goal of a united Germany. Yet this was met with some pessimism by other western countries, particularly France and England whom had not forgotten about the horrors of 2 World Wars perpetrated by the Germans. Israel was also leery about the thought of a unified Germany, fearing that it would imperil the Jewish people. However, most Germans living in both East and West Germany supported reunification. In the mean time, the GDR would attempt to establish some reforms, but when the FRG gave them an ultimatum to allow free elections or risk being denied financial aid, the GDR gave in and held elections in March of 1990 which were won by the conservative Alliance for Germany, bringing an end to socialist rule in East Germany. The Alliance for Germany would form the interim government in East Germany until reunification of East and West Germany.

In December of 1989, delegates from France, Britain, the United States and the Soviet Union met at the Allied Control Council Building in Berlin to discuss an independent Germany. Everyone agreed that Germany should be allowed unification, independence and self-determination, and that the existing borders in Europe be respected. The only point of contention was concerning the German military. Gorbachev initially objected to Germany remaining a part of NATO and the EC, and predicated his agreement on the overall matter to Germany remaining neutral. Many in the Soviet government considered the East German military as integral to the Soviet's armed forces. But when economic turmoil and unrest began to take shape in the Soviet Union, Gorbachev decided to concede on the Germany/ NATO issue and accept the condition that Germany remain in NATO. The West German government immediately set aside 12 Billion marks to help facilitate the reunification process, which required the construction of housing and the vacating of over 100,000 Soviet Union soldiers back to the Soviet Union. In September of 1990, Germany, the US, the Soviet Union, France, and Britain signed the Two plus Four Treaty which ended allied occupation of Germany and set in motion its official reunification. The next step was currency unification. The East German mark, the currency of GDR was still in circulation but declining in value, and the West German mark(the Deutschmark) was spreading eastward. Another thing was that many east Germans were still migrating westward. Economists at that that time believed that the way to stop the endless migrating would be by unifying the currencies and also restricting east German access to west German social benefits. It was believed that by restricting benefits to east German migrants in West Germany, the West German government could influence east Germans to be more insistent on remaining in place in East Germany. On the currency unification issue, however, some wanted for the two currencies to be valued at a 1 to 1 exchange rate, meaning one West German mark would equal one East German mark. This was proposed for the sake of preventing citizens in East Germany from having their savings wiped out. Ultimately, it was agreed that a 1:1 exchange rate would apply to a certain amount of savings, while a 1:2 exchange rate would apply to other amounts. This agreement was ratified in May of 1990 and officially in place in July of 1990.

The two German states unifying had been the first time such an amalgamation had occurred. Never before has a capitalist society merged with a communist society to become one. A number of issues were initially encountered. For example the historically low productivity rates of East Germany compared to West Germany lowered Germany's overall labor market performance after the two countries united. Only 2 years after unification, the industrial productivity plummeted 73% from the levels reached in 1989. These challenges persisted even as the influence of eastern Europe and Soviet Union over East Germany was quickly dissipating. Just prior to the unification, West Germany began taking steps to privatize the GDR's economy. One way of attempting to achieve this involved taking over a Trust Agency in East Germany called Treuhand, which was initially formed by the GDR for the purpose of reallocating East German firms to new management. This was the state's way of facilitating privatization. The Trust would take on the assets and liabilities of roughly 8000 East Germany companies and sell them to private individuals who were bidding on the firms. This measure, even after East Germany was drifting away from communism, was met with disdain by some who retained a socialistic outlook. The CEO of this Trust would end up being assassinated at his home by a sniper in 1991.

Another issue of unification that came to the forefront was the issue of property rights. The vast expropriations of property imposed by the East German government under the GDR socialist state from 1949 - 1989 made it difficult for the FRG to figure out who the original owners of the property were. Millions of claims were made and confirmed, nevertheless. And this would ultimately scare off investors looking to get into the real estate market.

There was also the wage issue which was exacerbated by the fact that the conversion rate of the East German mark to the West German mark kept production costs elevated, and wages dispersed would exceed what the corresponding productivity had warranted. Thus, West German companies would try to integrate their new East German markets by simply establishing more production facilities in the western part of Germany as opposed to the eastern part. But it wasn't just the wage issue that deterred west German companies from expanding their operations into East Germany. East Germany had been plagued with deprecating and degraded infrastructure, along with energy shortages, which affected communication lines such as telephone service. A number of east German power grids were shut down as a result of this energy shortage, which posed a safety issue. Many of the streets and railways in East Germany were in such bad condition, that they had to undergo serious renovation, and many of them had to be rebuilt. This was also the case for the autobahns. All of these issues underscored a serious delay in the unification process of transitioning East Germany from a socialist state to a free-market economy, and it became the case that measures which were enacted to speed up the process could be something that would ultimately obstruct long term economic growth. It was believed that an efficient transition could only happen if the expected initial fallback would be allowed to occur, as opposed offering compromises to keep such events from happening, compromises that could create permanent burdens on the structure of the economy. At the same time, though, there is a dilemma here that German economists had to contend with, such that allowing disruptions could result in the type of devastation that could impede and even jeopardize both the economic and political stability needed for setting in motion a smooth transition. Upheaval could further exacerbate the exodus of East Germans from East Germany to West Germany. Trying to find a middle ground on dealing with these issues was usually more expensive, and trying to cut the cost of the transition by allowing certain outcomes to happen was something that presented possible obstruction to the whole process altogether.

The conservative model welfare state that existed in the FRG prior to the unification was much more sustainable because it was not burdened by the prospect of increased costs that integration with East Germany brought about. These costs involved matters pertaining to fixing infrastructure problems in East Germany, dealing with the migration issue—West Germany needed to find a way to incentivize people to stay in East Germany, and the labor issue—labor market productivity in East Germany was inferior than what it was in West Germany. West Germany's financial system was one that offered social welfare programs, but based on worker output, collective taxation of wage earning employees, and GDP.

This type of system is contingent on a labor market comprised of high productivity and high employment. This is was the case in West Germany, but not East Germany and created some problems in the unification transition process. In West Germany, when it came to insurance, workers normally allocated part of their salary for taxation, while their employees would match their contribution. The sum would be pooled into a national pool that would handle meeting insurance claims. The East German economic backdrop of high unemployment and low productivity combined with increasing demands for social benefits was a drain on the German economic system, since in that case of high unemployment in East Germany, worker contributions would also be lower. West Germany was thus forced to take up the slack amid this lack of taxed contributions and increased insurance claims among the less productive demographic of workers in Eastern Germany. The increasing costs of accommodating this declining contribution/beneficiary ratio into the German economy pressured the West German government to enact reforms on welfare spending. By 1995, the unemployment rate in East Germany had grown significantly and was 2 times higher than it was in West Germany. Not to mention that the number of welfare recipients had also increased to exceed the number of wage-earning workers nationally. By the year 2000, social welfare spending comprised of 32% of the national GDP, and 50% of the GDP in East Germany. Germany exceeded the deficit limits established in the Stability and Growth Pact, which was part of the Maastricht Treaty—an agreement between a number of European countries to cooperate politically and economically. This agreement is what has come to be known as the European Union(EU). It developed out of the European Commission. The Stability and Growth pact that was established concurrently with the formation of the EU was aimed at setting limits on how much European countries in the EU can spend. According to the agreement, the budget deficit could not exceed 3% of the GDP, and the national debt could not surpass 60% of the GDP.

Regardless of these issues, the transition of unification did get rolling by way of a determined East Germany. The Treuhand had been made up of employees from West Germany and was endowed with such responsibility, that it was basically the governing body for East Germany. Much of the investment into East Germany was by west German investors, and those non-German firms that did invest into eastern Germany were companies that had subsidiaries in West Germany. The state of East Germany was of such a condition that it became very difficult for Treuhand to lure foreign investment into that region. Consequently and unexpectedly, East Germany's economy had declined considerably in the ensuing years after reunification; unemployment jumped past 3 million, and industrial production plummeted. In 1991, overall production in East Germany

comprised just a mere 8% of West Germany's total production output that year.

The transition process was largely facilitated by west Germans, and for that very reason, many of the firms in East Germany were just subsidiaries of west German companies. And these subsidiaries followed the same company models of their parent company in the west, in terms of ownership and management. The assets of banks in East Germany were assumed by west German banks, whom would place their own western bank reps in management and board positions at the banks in East Germany, allowing western firms to maintain control over the operations there. The Treuhand was set up in this manner, where many of its employees would be from banks in West Germany. The initial problems associated with a transition of unifying East and West Germany into one sovereign state slowed down the pace of economic growth. Very little investment flowed into East Germany during the early stages of unification. In fact, capital inflows to East Germany only made up 1% of the national GDP. And much of this inflow was relegated simply to investors purchasing the companies there. It was clear that a lot more was required for not just investing in ownership, but also renovating and rehabilitating those firms. But investors were cautious, buying the firms and making sure that the company would be functional in terms of productivity before committing more investment towards wages and renovations. Many investors backtracked on their commitments to the east German firms. Because much of West Germany's expenditures were allocated to infrastructure and social benefit payments to the unemployed, disabled and elderly in East Germany, less would available for investment into further economic development. The infrastructure projects certainly helped in terms of job creation but did little to contribute to overall growth of the economy. A short-term fallback was noted when it came to why. It was presumed that the time dedicated to training employees cut into the time employees would spend seeking employment. Moreover, in terms of spending, it was concluded that the German government spent 350 billion Deutschmarks on the economic, monetary, and unification process in East Germany over the course of the first 3 years. Between 1992 and 1995, Germany would spend nearly 850 billion Deutschmarks on East Germany. When taking into account the population in East Germany, such expenditure could have payed every person living in East Germany 50,000 Deutschmarks. This underscores just how adamant and insistent the west German government was about unification.

During the first stage of unification, West Germany's economy improved somewhat, largely in part to the demand created by people coming into the country from eastern Germany. Unlike East Germany's economy, which declined significantly immediately after

unification, West Germany's GDP rose roughly 4.6% in 1990. That same year, the cost of living managed to remain steady even as wages increased in some industries. Employment rose during that year, and unemployment dropped, and this was likely due to the influx of workers coming in from East Germany filling vacant job openings. The unemployment rate would thus decline to 7%. Between 1990 and 1991, nearly 400,000 people from East Germany were commuting to their jobs located in the west. Another factor in the GDP growth was that many east Germans wanted to acquire goods from West Germany, goods they considered superior to the ones produced in East Germany. Many in East Germany also deposited their money in West German banks, increasing the inflow of capital there, which was another positive influence on the economy in the west. Despite these aspects which were conducive to economic growth in the western part of Germany, the Bundesbank had become concerned that the stimulus of capital flowing into the west from the east would pose an inflationary risk. There was also heightened worry about increasing government deficits as a result of infrastructure spending on east Germany. These prospects made it clear to the banking industry in western Germany that interest rates would have to remain elevated in order to mitigate the risk of high inflation from West Germany's rapid growth rate and money supply increase. This fear of price hikes led the banks to increase short term interest rates sharply between 1991 and 1992. The average short term interest rate spiked from 7.1% in 1989 to 8.5% in 1990, before rising to 9.2% and 9.5% in 1991 and 1992 respectively. It wasn't until 1993 that the Bundesbank allowed rates to decline, during which time they would fall to 7.3%. The bank was confident that the inflationary pressures were held in check by that point. Following these monetary policy measures, the rate of growth in western Germany began to slow down; in the last quarter of 1992, West Germany's economic growth rate was barely 1%--a far cry from where it was in the first quarter of 1991 at 4.2%. Comprehensively in 1992, the growth rate would total 1.5% from the year before, indicating a slowdown of the growth rate by 3.7%. In eastern Germany, the growth rate there would fall below analyst expectations. It was anticipated that 1992 would bring at least a 7% growth rate, but the official numbers turned out to be just 6%. Both East and West Germany saw an increase in unemployment in 1992; the total unemployed in Germany that year was a record 4 million people. West Germany made up two-thirds of that number, while East Germany made up one-third. But nevertheless, the national GDP for all of Germany that year had risen above 3 trillion Deutschmarks. East Germany contributed 7% of that. The slowdown of the growth rate continued into 1993, going negative -1.2%. After having cut short term rates for over a year, Germany's economic growth rate would begin to steadily rise on average roughly 2% a year from that point. Unemployment also begin to drop, albeit slowly and gradually.

Ultimately, the unification process had come with a large trade off requiring West Germany to invest around 2 trillion marks for the purpose of developing the east German economy, transitioning it from a socialist state to a social market economy. The costs of rehabilitating the infrastructure there made up a considerable portion of that 2 trillion mark investment. But time would indicate that eastern Germany could never catch up with West Germany's economic efficiency. Even by 2011, the results showed that the growth rate was still trailing that of West Germany's. Unemployment remained much higher in the east, a result that many economists blamed on West Germany's subsidization of eastern Germany's societal infrastructure. The complacency in eastern Germany is considered to have been brought on by excess expenditures by the west German government on unemployment benefits, welfare, and job security measures in the east. The economic miracle that began shortly after World War II in West Germany had dissipated by the early 2000s. The costs of reunification which ultimately slowed down the German economy from the pinnacles it reached during the economic miracle led to Germany becoming ridiculed as "the sick man of Europe." In 2003, the German economy underwent a brief recession, during a time when the economic growth rate was only averaging 1.2% annually between 1988-2005. High unemployment continued to plague the east German economy regardless of the government spending on social programs there. In 2008, the worldwide financial crisis impacted Germany's GDP, causing it to decline. But as it turned out, Germany's economy recovered faster from the 2008 financial crisis than any other nation, and this momentum would carry over into 2010 and beyond as global demand reinvigorated Germany's export markets, which would account for half of the German GDP.

The euro began as a virtual currency in 1999, after having been proposed over the past few decades prior. It was a longstanding goal for the European coalition movement since the 1960s, and later for the EU in the 1990s. The Maastricht Treaty came about in 1993 with the very intention of establishing an economic and monetary union for EU member states by 1999. The UK was excluded from this goal, as well as was Denmark. By 2002, euro notes and coins entered circulation and quickly took precedence over the other national currencies that were circulating at the time. In retrospect, discourse about a monetary union for European countries goes back to the League of Nations, proposed by Woodrow Wilson at the end of World War I. Even back then, a unified currency under what was called the Latin Monetary Union was proposed for France, Italy, Belgium and Switzerland. Later, policy makers would devise a way to formulate a similar framework. The first initiative on this matter was conducted in 1969 by the European Commission(EC), whose goal was to express a necessity for Europe to coordinate on economic and monetary cooperation. Shortly thereafter, a conference among the European Council at the Hague discussed ways to reduce exchange rate volatility. This meeting led to a proposal—which would be published in 1970 by Pierre Werner, who was the Prime Minister of Luxembourg—that advised for a centralized macroeconomic policy making-framework which would fix the fluctuation of European currencies and make the movement of capital less restricted. When the US took the US dollar off the Bretton Woods Gold Standard in 1971, the widespread currency devaluation that followed curtailed the goals of monetary unity set forth by the European Commission. But in 1979, the European Monetary System(EMS) was established and fixed exchange rates to an accounting unit called the European Currency Unit(ECU). The purpose was to counter exchange rate fluctuations and inflation. The European Monetary Cooperation Fund would later come out of the EMS. In 1988, the European Council developed a plan for monetary unity which was supported by France, Italy and the European Commission. European Commission President Jacques Delores was then asked in 1989 to head up a committee of central bank governors that would be tasked with formulating the concrete methodology towards the development of an economic and monetary union (EMU). His draft put forth a blueprint for the EMU in three phases, one which would establish the European System of Central Banks(ESCB)--an institution that would oversee the creation and implementation of monetary policy. The first stage of this blueprint was liberalizing capital movements in the European economic community by getting rid of exchange controls. The was followed by the Maastricht Treaty of 1992 which established an agreement on monetary union, setting the path for a single currency for EU member states, except the UK. This single currency was slated to go into effect by 1999. At first, Germany was somewhat apprehensive about parting ways with the DeutscheMark. France on the other hand approved the treaty, while the UK and Denmark decided to abstain. In 1992, the UK's currency, the pound sterling, had briefly collapsed and was forced to withdraw from the EMS.

The second phase of Delors's plan started in 1994 with the European Monetary Institute, formed to phase out the European Monetary Cooperation Fund which was developed out of the EMS. The European Monetary Institute would directly precede the European Central Bank. At the a conference of the European Monetary Institute in 1995, the euro was created and was to be the name of the new currency that would replace the former accounting currency, European Currency Unit (ECU). The launch date was set for January 1, 1999. Back in 1997, the European Council ratified the Stability and Growth Pact which set rules on how much EU member states governments could spend. The Pact was meant to ensure fiscal discipline after the euro would be launched in 1999. The ERM II was also established as the exchange rate mechanism between the euro and the national currencies of countries that may enter the eurozone later on.

In 1998, the third stage of Delors's plan involved the selection of 11 member countries that would qualify to adopt the euro in what would be called the eurozone. The prerequisites required for each country to maintain a budget deficit lower then 3% of their national GDP, a national debt level less than 60% of the national GDP, low inflation, and interest rates within the average EU rates. Greece was the only country excluded from the eurozone in January 1999 because they failed to meet those requirements. (They would however later join the eurozone in 2001, thanks to Goldman Sachs.) At the end of the implementation of all 3 of Delors's phases for establishment of a united currency system under the euro, the European Monetary Institute was set to be replaced by the European Central Banks. It had been established in June of 1998 that the European Central Bank would replace European Monetary Institute after the euro would go into effect in January of 1999. It would be then that conversion rates would be established between the euro and those national currencies of the 11 member countries in the EU that comprised the eurozone. The rates were put in place on a recommendation basis provided to the Council of the EU from the European Commission, and it would be based on market rates on the last day of 1998, so that a 1:1 exchange rate would exist between the European Currency Unit and the euro. The reason it had to be the rates from December 31, 1998 was because the European Currency Unit "depended on the closing exchange rate of the non-euro currencies (principally the pound sterling) that day. Due to differences in national conventions for rounding and significant digits, all conversion between the national currencies had to be carried out using the process of triangulation via the euro."

The euro became official when the national currencies of the 11 member countries in the eurozone were no longer independent but fixed to each other. The euro was initially launched in virtual form and transacted mostly through electronic means, but eventually replaced the other national currencies in 2002 when euro coins and banknotes were released into circulation. In January of 1999, all bonds and government debts of the 11 EU member countries in the eurozone became denominated into euros. The euro started out already exceeding the value of the US dollar. In January of 1999, the euro was worth 1.16 US dollars. The Deutschmark, which was anticipated to trade concurrently with the euro at the start of

January quickly disappeared right after the markets opened. The US dollar would gain ground and go on par with the value of the euro by the end of 1999, which led to emergency measures by the European Central bank to prop up the euro. Member countries of the EU were given a deadline to revoke the legal tender status of their national currencies by February 28, 2002, 2 months after euro coins and banknotes were released into circulation. Germany revoked the legal tender status of the Deutschmark on December 31, 2001, unlike other member countries that waited until the deadline to remove their national currency's legal tender status. In some countries, the exchangeability of the national currency would remain in place until June 30, 2002. For other nations like Germany, Austria, Ireland, and Spain, the national banks there continued to exchange the national currency beyond the June 2002 deadline. In Germany, Deutsch Telekom altered the payment system for 50000 payphones, making them available for accepting Deutschmark coins in 2005.

Over the years after the institution of the euro in 1999 and its brief decline in early 2002, the euro would gradually recover, increasing in value relative to the dollar, and by 2008, one euro would become worth $1.59. The euro's value also increased against the pound sterling in the late 2000s. Former chairman of the Federal Reserve Alan Greenspan forecasted in 2007 that the euro would eventually surpass the importance of the US dollar.

In response to the worldwide financial crisis of 2008 that impacted the EU growth rate negatively, the Lisbon Treaty was established and aimed to foster even greater economic cooperation in Europe by formalising what is called the Eurogroup, a conference of euro finance ministers headed by Jean-Claude Juncker. Germany, however, was skeptical about the efforts of the Eurogroup, believing that it would challenge the sovereignty of the European Central Bank. Just prior to the establishment of the Eurogroup, the leaders of eurozone EU member states met in Paris to discuss the problems arising from the 2008 financial crisis, and it was there where progress was made in discussing measures for responding to the recession. The plan that would come about amounted to over one hundred billion euros that would be injected into the financial system in order to prevent a total collapse. The plan consisted of governments buying up a stake in various banks in order to help raise the banks's finances and facilitate interbank lending. The EU considered cooperation on this matter to be imperative since the prospect of nations going rogue could have made the banking sector's credit issues much worse. And many investors in the EU feared that the 2008 crisis could trigger a possible dissolution of the eurozone. But ultimately, the eurozone recovered quite considerably over the course of 2009 as bond yield spreads between Germany and the less efficient economies in the eurozone had declined. Many credited this aversion of catastrophe on the actions of the European Central Bank, which injected 500 billion euros into the banking sector in June of 2009. Thus the euro would garner a reputation of being safe investment, leading to more European countries applying to become part of the EU.

Despite the bailout by the European Central Bank, Greece and few other member states were in danger of going into default due to the fact that they were still struggling to raise funds. This led to eurozone leaders establishing a plan called the European Financial Stability Facility, and it was created to bail out the struggling member nations in the eurozone. It was backed by funds from the IMF and help from the European Financial Stabilization Mechanism. The debt crisis would compel further urgency among European leaders to push for more European integration. According to the website of the European Commission https://ec.europa.eu/ "The European Financial Stabilisation Mechanism (EFSM) was created for the European Commission to provide financial assistance to any EU country experiencing or threatened by severe financial difficulties. The EFSM was used to provide financial assistance conditional on the implementation of reforms to Ireland and Portugal between 2011 and 2014, and to provide short-term bridge loans to Greece in July 2015."

The European Financial Stability Facility's(EFSF) lending capacity of 400 billion euros could be combined with loans from the European Financial Stabilization Mechanism amounting to a max of 60 billion euros, and loans from the IMF at a max of 250 billion euros. The EFSC went into operation in 2011 for the purpose of bailing out Ireland and Portugal. Member states of the EU could request support from the European Commision and the IMF by presenting a fiscal plan that would have to be approved by the Eurogroup. Initially, the country requesting assistance would meet with representatives from the International Monetary Fund and the European Central Bank and a support program would be drawn up and sent to the Eurogroup for approval. Once the program is approved, the EFSF would provide the loan to the country in need. This would take several days as the EFSF would need time to raise the funds. The amounts dispersed are based on metrics used by the ECB, and the guaranteed amounts to be lent increased from 440 billion euros to 780 billions euros, an increase that would ultimately burden the more fiscally sound member countries of the EU, should one of the member countries default on a EFSF loan. The 2010 bailout of Greece was not part of this EFSF guarantee, but part of another arrangement that involved eurozone countries and the IMF.

Greece was able to become part of the eurozone with the help of Goldman Sachs, an American investment firm. Despite an inability to meet the fiscal requirements of the Stability and Growth Pact,

Greece was able to join the eurozone in 2001 through a technique that would mask the government's debt load through currency swaps. Goldman Sachs provided to Greece a secret loan of 2.8 billion euros which was disguised as a "cross-currency swap." This complicated transaction artificially wiped out 2% of Greece's national debt, allowing them to present themselves as eligible to join the eurozone. But when this trick was revealed in 2009, Greece's deficit turned out to be worse than indicated with its national debt comprising 127% of the GDP. The EU decided to intervene and a troika consisting of the European Commission, the European Central Bank and the IMF provided Greece with a 110 billion euro loan to pay off creditors and also adhere to austerity measures such as higher taxes and lower spending so that Greece could grow back into a surplus. The austerity measure however did not produce the intended result. Greece's national debt would grow to 172% of the GDP by 2011. The troika would provide Greece with another bailout of 130 billion euros and further measures to get Greece to comply with austerity measures. This second attempt would be more successful and Greece would began to come out of their debt problems. However, the austerity measures were creating domestic problems, such as rising unemployment and a decline in wages, which would lead to a snap election in Greece in 2015 where the people of Greece would vote into power someone who would do away with the austerity measures. The Prime Minister of Greece demanded for restructuring with the troika, but the increased spending caused Greece to fall further into debt and eventually defaulting, missing a 1.6 billlion payment due to the IMF. As Greece shut down its stock market, they would finally give into a third bailout/austerity plan offered by the EU, but to this day Greece is sill marred by severe debt problems as a result of their fiscal mismanagement.

Chapter 7: The End of the Rublezone

After the Soviet Union broke up in 1991, Russia and other former Soviet states were looking to figure out what would be the best course of action in terms of currency—remaining within the rublezone or introducing one own national currency. Introducing a currency unique to the country was often a testament to the country's sense of pride, independence, and sovereignty. It also gave a country the necessary backdrop to pursue an independent monetary policy. Much as it was over in western Europe, the former Soviet states in eastern Europe were tempted to avoid multi-national economic integration by issuing a national currency. This sentiment was perhaps stronger in eastern Europe, considering the fact that many of the former Soviet states were eager to breakaway from a bloc that had been largely described as oppressive. Multilateral cooperation was somewhat of a longstanding goal for western Europe. But for eastern Europe states outside of Russia, such was a been-there/done-that perspective, and by 1993, most former Soviet states were gearing up to establish their independent currency. Kyrgystan, Latvia, Estonia, and Lithuania were pretty dead set on establishing a single national currency for their respective country. Later that same year, Georgia, Moldova, and Azerbaijan were on the same path to independent currency. However, Ukraine and Belarus, as east Slavic nations along with Russia, were slower to embark upon the path of monetary independence, preferring to correspond with Russia on more steady withdrawal from the rublezone. Turkmenistan would later announce its goal to pursue monetary independence. Armenia, Kazakhstan, Uzbekistan remained undecided, while Tajikstan stated its desire to remain in the ruble zone.

While establishing a single national currency has its benefits, it also comes with drawbacks; one in particular is costs, and sometimes this may outweigh the benefit of independent currency. There is no guarantee of economic success by choosing to go the independent route in terms of monetary policy because much of it is contingent on the country's capabilities, skills, and knowledge. We saw in the case of Germany, especially West Germany that there was no shortage of educated and skilled workers often times willing to work for lower wages. Moreover, when it comes to the costs of establishing monetary reform, much of the success of meeting those costs depends on timing and other factors like fiscal management and labor mobility. Exchange rate may also serve as a factor that stabilizes output. Of course, there is the conflict of interest where an appreciating value in the national currency can diminish a nation's competitive viability in some export markets.

After the Soviet Union collapse, a number of Russian reformers were eager to break up the ruble zone but met considerable resistance, as fifteen independent central banks began issuing increasingly more ruble credits, which led to hyperinflation between 1992 and 1993. By late 1993, most former Soviet states had left the rublezone, and those countries that departed earlier fared better economically than those who did not. When the Soviet Union broke up into 15 independent states, each of those states had its own central bank that would continue to issue ruble credits. And this was problematic because none of the banks were putting limits on their money issuance since they all assumed that the other central banks continued to issue large credits. The rublezone would thus become hyperinflationary, and this did not curtail support for the zone. The only detractors were First Deputy Prime Minister Yegor Gaidar and the Baltic leaders. Gaidar actually wanted Russia to nationalize the ruble, and so did many of Russia's western advisors. But nations that were on the best of terms with Russia, such as Belarus, Kazakhstan, Armenia, and Tajikistan wanted the rublezone to continue. Those other nations that were eager to distance themselves from Russia, such as Ukraine, Moldova, Georgia, Azerbaijan, Turkmenistan, and Uzbekistan were all looking forward to setting up their own national currency. Russia's major concern in this regard was the fact that in the event that other states leave the rublezone and create a national currency, the remaining rubles in those countries could flow into Russia, causing an increase in the money supply of rubles in Russia, thereby further exacerbating inflationary prospects.

In 1992 and 1993, Russia continued to export its energy products to former Soviet states at subsidized prices. But when countries departed the rublezone, Russia had discontinued selling their oil to them at those discounts. The Baltic states which left the eurozone the earliest saw a significant increase in energy prices that Russia was charging them, to the point where they would go from buying Russian oil at discounts to buying Russian oil at world market prices. It was almost an 80% difference. A decline in the terms of trade with Russia was certainly a drawback for former Soviet states leaving the rublezone, but the Baltics were convinced that a national currency was border fence to Russia. Other entities that maintained favorable sentiments about the former establishment wanted the rublezone to remain in place. Many large companies wanted to conduct commerce without serious competition, and be paid through a central bank. It was also the case that many international entities like the EU were in favor of the rublezone remaining in place as they were eager to establish a joint currency zone for Europe, even though such was untenable. This was perhaps indicative of European interests at the time, which was seeking to find alternate methods of banking without centralization. But this was likely a far-fetched goal since it was normally maintained that monetary efficiency is only possible though a central bank that would issue the currency. But in Russia at this time right after the break-up of the Soviet Union, there were 15 different central banks embarking on a very fast-paced monetary expansion. Each bank realized that the more rubles they issued, the greater the share of the GDP they would account for. But as the ruble supply increased, prices went higher and inflation would grow. In 1992, inflation was between 640 and 3000% among former Soviet states. Among those nations remaining in the rublezone, inflation was as high as 11000% in 1993. Those Baltic states that departed the zone in the summer of 1992 were able to avoid the extremes of an inflationary scenario since with an independent national currency, they could restrict the amount of credit they would issue. Other former Soviet state officials, however, lacked scholarship on currency economics and believed that credit was not money, and because of this, they assumed they could simply reduce the amount of money printing in order to curtail rising inflation. But the printing machines were only in Russia. The other former Soviet states had to make do with what they had in terms of notes still circulating their economy. Thus, when inflation occurred, they would be left with serious cash shortages as prices increased. As a result, many of the non-Russian former Soviet states began printing their own substitute ruble currencies. Yet this did not lead to radical intervention in monetary policy. Russia maintained account surpluses with all the former Soviet states and provided most of their financing. The central banks of these former Soviet states would normally repay their debts to Russia by issuing more ruble credits. According to the IMF, in 1992, Russia's financing made up 91% of Tajikistan's GDP and 70% of Uzbekistan's GDP. For Turkmenistan, Georgia, and Armenia, Russia's financing accounted for about 50% of their GDPs. For Belarus and Moldova, Russia's financing only accounted for 10% of their GDPs. This level of financing had become unsustainable for Russia, who was dealing with their own financial problems. Russia would thus implement monetary tightening measures and restrict credits to those nations. Such led to an arrears crisis. Arrears are inter-enterprise debts. The backdrop of this crisis is understood through the Soviet Union centralized payment system, in which every payment would have to go through the central bank. At one point, the number of enterprises in the Soviet Union were minimal, which is why there was a limit on the number of payments, but as the amount of enterprises in the Soviet Union grew, an increase in payment delays coincided with it. Normally, state-owned enterprises were certain that the state would eventually come around to clearing their inter-enterprise debt. These debts continued to rise because the enterprises would continue to produce and sell the supplies and at times not expect immediate payment in return, assuming that the state would eventually come around to paying them. Many times these arrears were orchestrated for purpose of extracting money from the government, essentially asking the central bank for a monetary emission. And under the planned economy of the old Soviet Union, this was typically how the system operated. When Russia began money-tightening implementations, these enterprises were not able to find buyers, and many of these enterprises were energy consuming and reliant on raw materials. Because of this, when they could not find buyers for their supplies, they would thus not have the money to purchase energy supplies needed for production. Normally, these enterprises would request a cash injection from the central banks, but at the time in early 1992, Russia was trying to tighten its fiscal policies. As the arrears crisis worsened, the central banks were left with no option but to soften their monetary policies, which led to high inflation. In January of 1992, inter-enterprise debts in Russia totaled around 37 billion rubles, and by July of that same year, the volume of inter-enterprise debt had risen to 3.2 trillion. The arrears crisis would have systemic implications for the Russian economy as the governor of Russia's Central Bank, Georgy Matyukhin, would be replaced by Viktor Gerashchenko. The inflation that came about from the intervention led to the resignation of Yegor Gaydar. Those measures put in place prior to July of 1992 which were intended to reduce the level of arrears may have been counter-intuitive, and many enterprise firms did not heed to those programs which urged for enterprises to adhere to hard budget constraints—covering their costs of production with income generated from sales of their product or from other financial sources. Because enterprises in the former Soviet states believed that their business will receive government subsidies in the future, inter-enterprise borrowing had become more widespread and took prominence over other forms of finance activity, and the resulting growth of such activity nearly collapsed the Russian economy. Inter-enterprise borrowing is a form of trade credit, which is not inherently a systemic problem to an economic system. For example, in the first quarter of 1992, US trade credit among non-financial institutions was 973 billion. In fact, when it comes to the industrial economy, enterprises borrow from their suppliers and clients quite regularly. But in the Soviet Union a number of businesses were government subsidized, and this made it easier for enterprises to borrow more, assuming they would be bailed out by the central bank at some point. In the US, in order to underscore the risk associated with an inter-enterprise loan, extremely high interest rates are charged. This is unlike Russia, where the interest rate on inter-enterprise borrowing was zero. The growth of inter-enterprise debts in Russia in 1992 stifled the monetary reforms that were intended to fix the economic problems.

As the Russian Central Bank (CBR) pushed forward with monetary expansion in response to the arrears crisis, it became apparent that the Russian Central Bank would not be able to continue financing the other former Soviet states. While the Russian government would attempt to intervene by restricting the expansion of credits, CBR governor Viktor Gerashchenko remained keen on the continued expanding of credits. However in April 1993, the Russian government stopped issuing technical credits to former Soviet states and only permitted for credits to be facilitated among government bodies but only from Russia's budget. In July of 1993, the rublezone came to an end when CBR governor declared that all Soviet banknotes would be worthless by the end of the month. This led to a panic in the former Soviet Union, and many people rushed to the banks to withdraw their old soviet banknotes so that they could hurry and purchase items before the value would expire at the end of July 1993. This marked the end of the rublezone as all the former Soviet states would withdraw from the rublezone and establish their own national currency. The only exception was Tajikistan, which was embroiled in internal strife, war, and conflict. The monetary failures of 1993 resulted in 7 of 12 former Soviet republics suffering higher inflation that they did in 1992. In 1994 and 1995, inflation would begin to dwindle, and looking back, one may consider that ending the rublezone worked out for the best. But in hindsight, the volatile transition leads one to think if the choas could have been avoided. The hyperinflation that ensued after the breakup of the Soviet Union ultimately crushed the economy. The GDP on average in the 12 former Soviet states plummeted 50%. The Baltic states, however, since they departed the rublezone the earliest only suffered a 44% drop on GDP. The poor planning that followed the Soviet Union breakup gave way to a 70% reduction in trade among the former Soviet states between 1991 and 1994. Romania and Bulgaria, while also suffering economically, would have suffered much worse had they not left the rublezone. It becomes clear when observing the Baltic states, that leaving the rublezone as quickly as possible was the best solution and would have prevented the economic disaster that occurred.

Currency zones like the rublezone are quite common. The EU has a eurozone and many small economies actually prefer to peg their currency to a large economy in order to avoid wild currency fluctuations. In fact, a bunch of independent currencies circulating on the market is the exception to the rule. Even the period of economic growth that occurred in the years prior to World War I consisted of two currency zones. One was the Latin Monetary Union which began in 1865 and lasted until 1927. The member nations of this union were France, Belgium, Italy and Switzerland, and later

Spain, Greece, Romania, Bulgaria, Serbia, and Venezuela. The other currency union was the Scandinavian Monetary Union which formed in 1873 and lasted until 1914. The nations that were part of that union were Sweden, Denmark, and Norway. Both unions collapsed when one of the nations within those unions devalued their currency. For the Latin Monetary Union, it was Greece. For the Scandinavian Monetary Union, it was Sweden. Both the Latin Monetary Union and the Scandinavian Monetary Union differed from the European Monetary Union in that the former's currency cooperation was based on the gold standard, and each country maintained its own central bank. Other examples of monetary unions are the East Caribbean Currency Union, the West African Economic and Monetary Union, and the Central African Economic and Monetary Community. The East Caribbean Currency Union was formed in 1983 and is comprised of 9 Caribbean states--Anguilla, Antigua and Barbuda, Dominica, Grenada, Montserrat, St. Kitts and Nevis, St. Lucia, and St. Vincent and the Grenadines. Their currency is pegged to the US dollar; and the union maintains a common central bank, The East Caribbean Central Bank. The central bank, however, in their case, does not implement any monetary policy.

The West African Economic and Monetary Union is composed of 8 West African countries, while the Central African Economic and Monetary Community consists of 6 member states. Both the Central African Economic and Monetary Community, along with the West African Economic and Monetary Union, as former French colonies, have been using the African franc since 1945 and both unions have a central bank–the Bank of Central African States and the Central Bank of the West African States. The African franc was previously pegged to the French franc before becoming pegged to the euro. It was devalued in 1948 and 1994.

We can reference these aforementioned examples and see pretty clearly that currency unions are quite common. And for the unions comprised of smaller countries, the common currency has been either based on the gold standard, the dollar, or the euro. Monetary Unions based on a fiat currency tend to take on a different approach. This was the case for the Austro-Hungarian Empire in 1918, Yugslavia in the year 1990, and the former Soviet states from 1991 – 1993. After World War I, the Austro-Hungarian empire was on a death spiral with no path to recovery. The remaining components of the central government had been financing themselves with vast money creation, and continued along this method even after the armistice was signed in November of 1918. In October, the very next month, Hungary would expand monetary emission, and a currency competition would ensue among Austro-Hungarian states. This is when Czechoslovakia, another Austro-Hungarian state, decided to stamp the notes circulating within their country after closing their borders. After doing this, Czechoslovakia imposed strict monetary policies and averted hyperinflation. Austria, Hungary, and Poland on the other hand took no serious monetary policy measures and would thus suffer severe hyperinflation.

Throughout the 1980s after the death of President Tito in 1980, Yugoslavia was slowly disintegrating amid an unstable economic system. Slovenia, Croatia, and 2 northern republics were maintaining account surpluses with Serbia. In 1991, the National Bank of Yugoslavia, which was managed by the Serbian government, increased monetary emissions for sake of Serbia's economy, and this hampered the value of Yugoslav dinar. Consequently, Slovenia immediately declared independence from the republic of Yugoslavia, much in part to protect its own financial health. Shortly thereafter, Yugoslavia waged war on Slovenia in a conflict that lasted 10 days, to which after was followed by Slovenia departing from the Yugoslavia republic. Slovenia cut ties from Yugoslavia, both politically and financially. Croatia would follow suit but ended up in a violent conflict with Serbia. In the mean time, hyperinflation marred the economies of the remaining countries in the Yugoslavia republic. Those nations were Bosnia and Herzegovina, and Serbia. This hyperinflation coincided with the collapse of the rublezone, and all together there would be 28 occurrences of hyperinflation among Austria-Hungary, Yugoslavia, and the USSR. This underscored the fact that breaking up a currencyzone comes with significant consequences. While the example of the Baltic states' departure from the rublezone indicates that a quick exit is recommended, there is still the possibility to geopolitical fallback as was the case when Slovenia sought independence from the Yugoslavia republic before being attacked by Yugoslavia. Many of the collapses were unexpected, and the subsequent chain of events were far more devastating than anyone could have predicted at that time. In this regard, one cannot discount those events as unrelated to contemporary time-frames. In fact, these currency zones of Austro-Hungary, Yugoslavia, and the Soviet Union were very similar to the current eurozone in the EU in that they were real monetary zones with both a common payment system and central bank, along with being comprised of multiple nation states. Therefore, all three in terms of their existence and destruction are very relevant to the eurozone. Being made of a joint central bank and payment system, these currency zones are set up in such a way that if one of the two fails, the economies which are impacted will encounter negative systemic outcomes. If the common payment system ceases to function, liquidity squeeze is likely to follow, which was case during the 2008 financial crisis when Lehman Brothers declared bankruptcy in September of that year.

One thing is clear, currency zones fail when there is no single central bank that is the sole issuer of currency. But even when this is established, competition can still arise among member states, leading to nations, which are part of a zone, opting to stamp their currencies and depart from the monetary union. Thus any central control must be held in place by a very solid consensus among member nations, otherwise, the zone is at risk of collapse. In those previous examples, the primary central bank disregarded their duties and behaved fiscally irresponsibly, which compelled the more fiscally responsible nations to depart from the zone in the name of self-defense. In the eurozone, the European Central Bank is the primary provider of euro banknotes, but demands for looser or tighter monetary policies by member states could challenge the European Central Bank's authoritative standing on monetary emission. This was the case for a number years when in it came to Germany, the number one economy in the eurozone. Because Germany's citizens have been more geared towards saving rather than spending, Germany has lashed out at the ECB for their loose monetary policies. Germany feared that the ECB's low interest rates would compromise savings and pensioner plans in Germany. If things escalated and Germany was to leave the eurozone, it can be predicted that their new currency would rally and exceed the value of the euro. Depending on the scale of the new currency's increasing value, Germany's export markets could take a serious hit. But on the domestic front, the stronger currency could be beneficial for things like domestic debt which would be denominated in a theoretically weaker euro. On the other hand, as we saw in the cases of Austro-Hungary, Yugoslavia, and the USSR(Soviet Union), the remaining member states in the eurozone would be subject to inflation risk as euros flow out of Germany into other EU member states, thereby increasing the money supply and inflation risk. For exiting member states of a currency zone, the risk is deflationary. Those remaining member states in the currency zone are essentially left at risk for hyperinflationary collapse.

The eurozone's common payment system is called Target 2 which is how central bank money is electronically transferred among the national central banks within the eurozone. The Target 2 systems keeps track of electronic euro transactions between central banks of nations in the eurozone. Up unto the euro crisis, Target 2 balances were settled via private interbank market. Prior to the time that Lehman Brothers declared bankrupcy, banks were able to offset declines in customer deposits by borrowing the corresponding amounts on the interbank markets. This is why Target 2 balances were not on the rise before 2008. The bankruptcy of Lehman brothers in 2008, however, created a great deal of mistrust in the interbank markets. The event has reduced the use of this mode of operation and is the starting point of the rise of the Target 2 balances. After the interbank's funding had dissipated in 2011, Target 2 balances increased in economically strong member states of the eurozone. The balances went negative in 8 of the southern member states. Because a lot of electronic euros were flowing into Germany due to the fact that Germany exports a lot to other member states who in turn pay Germany via electronic euros through the Target 2 system, Germany had thus made more claims against the European Central Bank which oversees the transactions between central banks in Target 2. Adding to these German claims against the European Central Bank was the fact that the Bundesbank was lending a lot of euros to eurozone nations with economic difficulties. Hans-Werner Sinn asserted that the common payment system of the eurozone was essentially acting as a bailout as the Bundesbank was lending money to those member nations of the eurozone experiencing financial hardship. Hans believes that the collapse of the eurozone amid high Target 2 balances would make it impossible for creditor nations like Germany to claim credits. This would thus lead to disputes as the eurozone has no contingency strategy for such a scenario. This is similar to what happened in Russia after the Soviet Union ended. Russia has made claims on rublezone credits that the central banks of former Soviet states were obligated to settle. When former Soviet states left the rublezone and established their own currency, Russia insisted that some of them meet their obligations to the Russian Central Bank via a pre-agreed exchange rate with their new currency. In any case, departures from a currencyzone may not sit well with other members especially if there are large unsettled obligations by the exiting country. In the eurozone, those payables reflected as electronic transfers in Target 2 are collateralized with other assets, such that in the event that one country departs from the eurozone, those assets backing the electronic transactions would cover some of the departing country's outstanding obligations.

The common payment system of the rublezone was something called Kartoteka II. It accounted for all payments within the rublezone, but ran into problems when the volume of payments increased and became unmanageable. Inter-enterprise debts began to accumulate in 1992 because enterprises would forego collecting payments if they knew they could garner subsidies from the state central banks. Enterprises were essentially allowing arrears to develop so that they could justify asking the central banks for monetary emission. Ultimately the central banks would agree to do so, and this is how inflation became out of control at that time. The Eurozone could have faced a similar threat had it not been for German resistance to loose monetary policy by the ECB. Because Germany is so well managed, much like the countries that departed

other currencyzone establishments, Germany too would economically benefit by exiting their respective currencyzone, the eurozone. Czechoslovakia's departure from Austro-Hungary, Slovenia's departure from Yugoslavia, and the Baltic states's departure from the USSR all benefited those nations economically and staved off much of the hyper-inflationary scenarios that affected the surrounding regions. If history is to repeat itself in the case of the eurozone, then Germany's eventual departure is not a matter of if, but when. However, some experts don't see Germany as the candidate to leave the eurozone since based on the previous examples, the nations that departed their respective currency zone were not just fiscally responsible, they were also small. So in this sense, some policy experts believe that should history repeat itself, it would be Finland that could depart the eurozone first since they operate as a benefactor, moreso than a beneficiary of the eurozone arrangement. And history shows that the country to exit a "currencyzone under duress" the quickest fares the best. This also underscores another risk arising from instability in the eurozone—nations could become more resolute to exit in order to meet that criteria for offsetting economic risk factors. An all or nothing solution is also possible, meaning that if a currency zone is facing collapse, it could be beneficial that every nation depart simultaneously.

Chapter 8: Bitcoin

The 2008 financial crisis and the subsequent bailout measures renewed pessimism about central banks and their monopoly on monetary emissions. The debates over the controversy of the 2008 bailout led to the creation of Bitcoin, and eventually scores of other digital assets. The fiat currencies of nation states met a potential competitor in Bitcoin and the crypto industry, which led to increased discourse about the possibility of a cashless society. This discussion about a cashless society actually goes back to the early formation of the internet over 20 years ago, and many economic experts and bankers back then ruminated about the possibility of information technology phasing out the need for central banks and paper money. Fast forward to today, the expansion of cryptocurrency has sparked renewed discussion about alternatives to cash and a lessened need for a central bank. But the volatility and risk associated with cryptocurrencies, as indicated by numerous instances of fraud, money laundering, crypto exchange collapses, and illegal activities, has given credence to arguments against the long-term sustainability of cryptocurrency. Nonetheless, central banks have felt increasing pressure from the rise of cryptocurrencies. Cryptocurrencies, according to June 2018 edition of the Finance and Development Journal, are "digital representations of value, made possible by advances in cryptography and distributed ledger technology. They are denominated in their own units of account and can be transferred peer to peer without an intermediary."

Bitcoin and cryptocurrencies' value is derived from the prospect of being able to use them to make purchases or exchange them for other fiat currencies. The latter is another factor that has allowed the US to continue with expansionary monetary policies, because Bitcoin's value is driven by the prospect that it can be exchanged for fiat currencies which in turn raises demand for fiat currency as Bitcoin holders would look to liquidate. This goes for both producers and consumers. Despite the threat of Bitcoin, a number of nations have yet to outlaw the cryptocurrency, and this likely because cryptocurrencies can prop up the value of fiat currency since many bitcoin holders do not see any value in the cryptocurrency other than the fact that it can be exchanged for legal tender at some point. Hence why nations are apprehensive about restricting it—in doing so they would disqualify their own currency from a demand that the bitcoin market fosters, and at the same time allow competing currencies of other nations to use Bitcoin to prop up the value of their national currency. This is likely how Russia got the ruble to recover so quickly following international sanctions imposed upon them after their invasion of Ukraine in 2022; they simply bought up scores of Bitcoin and liquidated them shortly after for rubles.

Another factor is that relatives of Russians living at a distance from the country could only send financial support to their relatives through bitcoin transactions. This influx of crypto likely correlated to a broadened demand for rubles, which in essence increased the value of it. Most nations are aware of how cryptocurrency can prop up the value of their national currency. And this will be the case as long as Bitcoin remains volatile.

On the other hand, a form of cryptocurrency called stablecoin, presents a real danger to national currencies because stablecoins are devised in such a way that investors would be more encouraged hold onto the cryptocurrency over a longer period of time. In stablecoin, volatility is considerably reduced, which would correlate to a lesser demand for fiat currency, a prospect that could turn cryptocurrencies into a direct competitor against fiat currencies. This is unlike non-stable volatile cryptocurrency, which is able to prop up fiat currencies due to the higher rates of liquidity demand. Stablecoins put central banks in a very precarious position. In late 2019, Facebook Inc announced its cryptocurrency initiative called Libra, which would be a "stablecoin" backed by various legal tender currencies, which mitigates the wild price fluctuation that currently afflict regular bitcoin/cryptocurrency. This announcement garnered a great deal of opposition from the global financial community because it could undermine/disrupt the current global financial system. Many countries have openly stated that Libra would be outlawed from being used in their country. Other countries have proposed to directly fight the Libra by starting their own government backed stablecoin. Instead of an open decentralized blockchain network of miners to verify the cryptocurrency transactions, the Libra cryptocurrency blockchain would have been managed by a private entity association, which gives even more rise to scrutiny. Such negative reaction to the initiative by international financial institutions led to Libra's demise shortly thereafter as Facebook would cancel in the initiative.

Chapter 9: Germany's Takeover of NATO and the European Central Bank

After the Russian invasion of Ukraine on February 24, 2022, German Chancellor Olaf Scholz announced Germany's intention to dial up their military spending, promising to allocate 100 billion euros to Germany's defense budget for 2022. Germany also agreed to reach the goal of dedicating 2% of their GDP to defense spending in order to meet NATO's criteria. The new spending initiative, Olaf announced in a session of Germany's parliament, would pay for an armaments project that would add to the German military arsenal. Scholz also stated that Germany would look to supply Ukraine with arms to help them fend off the Russian invasion. Scholz stated to the lawmakers in parliament, "In attacking Ukraine, [Russian President Vladimir] Putin does not just want to eradicate a country from the world map, he is destroying the European security structure." With the potential of Russia expanding its military aims, Germany has a greater sense of urgency in equipping themselves with the means to defend their security. This announcement came a year after Germany spent a record amount on building up its military capabilities in 2021. Much of this increased spending has come about not just in reaction to the Russian invasion, but also at the urging of other NATO members like the United States, who felt that Germany was not investing enough in defense. For a number of years, the US felt that it shouldered too much of the load when it came to NATO policy. Yet this move by NATO, not just to allow Germany to rearm itself, but also encourage them is a far cry from the fears that came about from German reunification after the collapse of the Soviet Union. Back then, many western countries were alarmed at the prospect, and now it is clear that the sense of urgency surrounding Germany as a geopolitical force has subsided. Because Germany has been a very fiscally conservative nation and the best economy in the eurozone, many lawmakers are critical of the move by Scholz to increase government spending.

If the next few years sees a Germany that is both carrying much of the load in the eurozone, both economically and militarily, it is possible that Germany's impatience with the European Central Bank(ECB) could increase in the coming years. The biggest complaint that Germany has had with the ECB is their continued insistence on soft monetary strategy. With prices on the rise in Germany as of 2022, the Bundesbank has become insistent that the ECB raise interest rates to reduce inflation risks. A rate hike, many argue, would strengthen the euro and bring down the cost of energy since most energy commodities are priced in US dollars. Germany's creditor strength in the eurozone combined with a growing ability to maintain the security of the eurozone will only add to its "institutional power" to steer the eurzone in accordance with Germany's own fiscal preferences. This is why Germany is likely in the future to use its bargaining power as the main creditor of the eurozone to garner more influence on ECB policy. Should this not manifest itself to some degree, Germany could become motivated to apply other measures in order to get the ECB to comply with the strategic aims of the Bundesbank. This is why it is likely that Germany would try to ensure 2 major outcomes before they would seek out a deal with Saudi Arabia in which Saudi Arabia would sell oil for euros in exchange for Germany backing Saudi Arabia militarily. These 2 major outcomes would involve cementing Germany's control over the European Central Bank, either through some form of policy agreement, eurozone member state referendum, or directly nationalizing the European Central Bank and the euro for what Germany would consider emergency purposes. As more customers in the eurozone nations move their euros away from their own country's central banks into the Bundesbank, Germany will accrue more claims against the ECB, which will further justify an argument that Germany should have more clout in influencing ECB policy.

Chapter 10: End of the US Unipolar Moment

When the Soviet Union collapsed in 1991, the US had become elevated to sole super power status. Since World War II up unto that time, the US could lay claim to vanquishing fascism and communism. And in order to affirms their status, the US would defeat the Iraqi army during the Gulf War in 1991 over a period of 5-6 weeks, impressive considering the fact that Iraq was the fourth largest armed forces in the world at that time, but yet completely crushed by the US army. America was untouchable and after the Soviet Collapse, the United States had free reign to impose its foreign policy agenda without any significant interference from another nation, now that Moscow was out of the way. Democracy was now the official justification of US foreign policy. When Bill Clinton became president shortly after the collapse of the Soviet Union, his administration began discourse on how the fall of the Soviet Union should benefit the United States. Many foreign policy pundits wanted the US to return to its old non-interventionist foreign policy and practice restraint. During Clinton's first tenure as president of the United States, a number of academics and professors from MIT wrote an article about US interests. In it, they asserted that an interventionist and globalist agenda was antithetical to US interests, arguing that multilateral relations pursued by the US overseas would only amount to minimal benefit. From their perspective, the US could benefit the domestic economy by contributing less militarily on the international front, thus saving money that could be used at home for issues like budget deficits, infrastructure, and race relations—all of which were less prioritized during the Cold War era. They felt that US involvement overseas would only lead to war weariness. Another factor mentioned in the article was regarding NATO, an international organization they felt had already served its purpose in deterring expansionary ambitions of the Soviet Union. Since it was the case that the Soviet Union collapsed, NATO no longer served any real purpose, which thus refuted the need for the US to continue its military backing of European countries. In this outlook, they argued that the US would shoulder the load for international security issues, even when direct US intervention would be unnecessary. Regardless of this urging from academia and scholars and foreign policy experts, the US continued to push forward with its internationalist agenda and worldwide promotion of democracy. Clinton continued to pursue the development of a multilateral foreign policy backed by the promotion of human rights and democratic values. He reached out to the United Nations and sought collaboration on peacekeeping efforts. While Clinton pursued an international framework where the US would use its military capabilities for intervention in

humanitarian crises, he did not want the US to unilaterally solve the world's problems. During Clinton's tenure, unwilling to have the US standby and witness overseas atrocities without doing anything, he ordered American military intervention in Somolia in 1993, Bosnia in 1995, and Kosovo in 1999. The US was also adamant about maintaining its geopolitical edge over other potential competitors like China and Russia, which cultivated a sense of urgency in the US to continue upgrading its military technology and capabilities. However, Clinton's opposition, the Republican party, was antagonistic to his multilateral approach, and when George W Bush ran for president in 2000, he vowed to remove the US from UN influence, and he also hated the idea that US troops should operate under the command of UN peacekeeping commanders. Bush preferred a foreign policy that was more unilateral in its approach, and he was also suspicious of the UN because he saw it as world order that could at some point interfere with US domestic policy. After Bush became president in 2000, he made it his objective to continue defense spending. He also wanted to challenge rising competitors and address nuclear proliferation issues by cracking down on rogue regimes who may be trying to acquire weapons of mass destruction. In September of 2001, in less than nine months into Bush's presidency, the US would experience one of the worst attacks on its own soil.

On September 11, 2001, terrorist hijackers of three commercial airliners that day took control of the planes and crashed them into the World Trade Center in New York City and the Pentagon in Washington DC, killing 3000 people. Among those killed were 372 foreigners, 138 of them from Latin America and the Caribbean. In the aftermath of the attacks, America found themselves appalled that such an attack could be carried out on US citizens, and many did not understand how such hate could be harbored against the United States. Some attributed the attack to extremist Islamic ideology, others to US foreign policy of having US soldiers based in Saudi Arabia following the Gulf War. The latter had become a serious offense to Muslims that regard Saudi Arabia as holy land, and US military presence there is one of the factors the conspirators of the 9/11 terrorist attacks used to justify their heinous actions on September 11, 2001. The other motive for the attack was outrage over US support of Israel in an ongoing conflict that has resulted in large scale civilian deaths. A week after the attacks, Bush held a joint session of Congress stating that it was hatred that motivated the attack, as Bush would say "They hate our freedoms: our freedom of religion, our freedom of speech, our freedom to vote and assemble and disagree with each other." Fear permeated Washington DC and many in the government felt that a second attack was more than likely to happen. But Bush did not support a passive strategy, preferring to go the pre-emptive route and push for reforms in US foreign policy. He established a new national security doctrine that would discard the former multilateral approach, and insert the unilateral approach. The doctrine also asserted a preemptive policy and the exportation of democratic values to the middle east in order to deter extremism. Within a month after the attacks, after giving Afghanistan an ultimatum to hand over Osama Bin Laden, the US invaded Afghanistan and Al Qaeda. In 3 months, the US drove out the Taliban and began a lone arduous 20 year process of trying to install a new pro-democratic government there, a task that would ultimately fail. Shortly afterwards in 2003, 2 years after the US invaded Afghanistan, Bush would launch an invasion of Iraq on the premise that Saddam Hussein was developing weapons of mass destruction. Despite lack of evidence from UN inspectors that such was the case, the US moved forward with the invasion regardless, justifying it by asserting that Saddam was trying to buy yellow cake uranium from West Africa. The US also chose not to seek UN approval for the invasion, which was right inline with Bush's initial platform for a unilateral approach that separates US policy from the UN's. The US would complete the overthrow of Saddam's regime in short order, but would face a long process of stabilizing the new Iraqi government against an insurgency of Al Qaeda offshoots and Saddam loyalists. Between Afghanistan and Iraq, the US spent billions of dollars in aid to stabilize the countries in the post-war era. But various factors like power struggles, corruption, and insurgency protracted US involvement and at times threatened to undo all the efforts aimed to democratize the region. A growing restlessness at home that saw no end in sight gave rise to a war weary sentiment that insisted a complete pullout of US forces from the region as quickly as possible. Americans became desperate for a change in US foreign policy and during the 2008 presidential election, Barack Obama presented a platform to the American public that revolved around bringing troops home, and moving forward with a foreign policy that would depart with direct US intervention in foreign conflict. Obama promised to withdraw US troops from Afghanistan and Iraq and also repair damaged US foreign relations which occurred as a result of previous foreign policy. He also stated his intention to restore the multilateral approach of cooperating with international organizations. This platform helped Barack Obama win the 2008 presidential election and in just eight months after he entered office, he would win the Nobel Peace Prize. And by the end of 2011, Obama withdrew US forces from Iraq. However, the Arab Spring in 2011 which provoked widespread protests throughout the Middle East and North Africa would challenge Obama's original platform of US non-intervention overseas. As these protests triggered violent government crackdowns on protesters in Libya and

Syria which led to numerous civilian deaths, pressure was put on the Obama administration to intervene in a growing human rights catastrophe. Obama would facilitate the overthrow of Gaddafi from Libya in 2011, despite Libya posing no imminent threat to the United States. NATO forces conducted airstrikes on various Libyan military posts, which caused more civilian casualties and gave rise to more extremism. The Obama administration then asserted regime change in Syria by recognizing the anti-government/anti-Assad rebels as the official governing authority of the country. Meanwhile, ISIS, a terrorist group made up of former Al Qaeda operatives, Iraqi insurgents, and Saddam loyalists, began embarking upon a series of attacks in Iraq and Syria after declaring a worldwide caliphate. Shortly thereafter, they managed to seize large swaths of territory in both nations. This led to US re-engagement, forcing the Obama administration to order airstrikes in Iraq and Syria in order to stop further destabilization of the region. The growing ISIS threat in Syria led to Russia sending military aid in form of air support in 2015 to back the Assad regime against the Syrian rebels and ISIS. Once again, the middle east had become a hotbed of violence and terror. Before long, both Libya and Syria would become a humanitarian catastrophe. US foreign policy during the Obama administration, despite its stated goals of pursuing diplomacy and better international relations, did little to resolve the middle east crisis. The administration would also set the stage for growing US tension with Russia.

At the 2008 NATO Summit in Romania, Vladimir Putin, president of Russia, used the event to state emphatically "The emergence of a powerful military bloc at our borders will be seen as a direct threat to Russian security." The US followed up at the same summit in 2008 with: "NATO welcomes Ukraine's and Georgia's Euro Atlantic aspirations for membership in NATO. We agreed today that these countries will become members of NATO." Thus, it was there when it became clear that Ukraine joining NATO was the primary flashpoint for Russia in their aggressive geopolitical policy towards Ukraine since 2014. Even back in 2008, France and Germany were also opposed to bringing those countries into NATO because its a European security issue, a fact that drew no sensitivity from the US. In retrospect, from 2000 to 2008, Russia put forth a western friendly foreign policy agenda, even flirting with the idea of joining NATO, which would have made Russia a military ally with the United States. Russia also signed on to a strategic partnership with the EU in 2000, stating Russia's intention to recognize the sovereign rights of Ukraine. However, the United States and NATO's illegal war against Iraq in 2003, and its aggressive and unfettered military interventions in Libya and Syria in 2011 alarmed the Russian state in what Russia felt was an audacious foreign policy

where the United States was attempting to position itself as an international police force. There was also a double standard that Russia felt the United States was applying by justifying their role in destabilizing Libya and Syria, asserting regime change, militarily aiding government opposition, and yet pointing out the moral implications of other countries looking to assert their own regional interests. This only served to confirm Moscow's suspicions of NATO. Russia believed that after the Cold War, NATO had no purpose since its initial establishment was not only for the sake of constraining German and Japan militarily, but also deterring any expansionist ambition of the Soviet Union after World War II. After NATO incorporated West Germany into the alliance, the Soviet Union, likewise, established the Warsaw pact with other eastern European countries, as well as East Germany in order to deter NATO expansion. But after the Soviet Union ended, the Soviets relinquished control over the alliance and effectively dissolved the Warsaw pact. In doing this, Russia was promised security guarantees from NATO, and Russia often stated that NATO has never fulfilled these promises and that NATO only continues to exist as a provocational entity, conducting aggressive military exercises near Russia's borders on a regular basis. All these factors, along with the fact that Ukraine had been entertaining the possibility of a military alliance with a multi-national military bloc (NATO), played a significant role in Russia's assertive policy against Ukraine in 2014 with the annexation of Crimea. Numerous foreign policy experts since the late 1990s warned about the dangerous implications of NATO expansion. Here is an excerpt from a May 2nd, 1998 interview with George F. Kennan by New York Times columnist Thomas Friedman. Kennan was a US diplomat during the Cold War and advocate of containment strategy: *"I think it (NATO expansion) is the beginning of a new cold war. I think the Russians will gradually react quite adversely and it will affect their policies. I think it is a tragic mistake. There was no reason for this whatsoever. No one was threatening anybody else. This expansion would make the founding fathers of this country turn over in their graves......."We have signed up to protect a whole series of countries, even though we have neither the resources nor the intention to do so in any serious way. [NATO expansion] was simply a lighthearted action by a Senate that has no real interest in foreign affairs. What bothers me is how superficial and ill informed the whole Senate debate was. I was particularly bothered by the references to Russia as a country dying to attack Western Europe....."Don't people understand? Our differences in the Cold War were with the Soviet Communist regime. And now we are turning our backs on the very people who mounted the greatest bloodless revolution in history to remove that Soviet regime. And Russia's democracy is as far*

advanced, if not farther, as any of these countries we've just signed up to defend from Russia. Of course there is going to be a bad reaction from Russia, and then [the NATO expanders] will say that we always told you that is how the Russians are — but this is just wrong."

This is an excerpt from a leaked diplomatic cable from Wikileaks in 2008 in which William Burns, U.S. Ambassador to Russia (2005-2008), is detailing the implications of admitting Ukraine into NATO: *NATO enlargement, particularly to Ukraine, remains 'an emotional and neuralgic' issue for Russia, but strategic policy considerations also underlie strong opposition to NATO membership for Ukraine and Georgia. In Ukraine, these include fears that the issue could potentially split the country in two, leading to violence or even, some claim, civil war, which would force Russia to decide whether to intervene,"*

From NATO's official website, a paper written in June 2000 entitled "NATO's Relations with Russia and Ukraine" written by R. Craig Nation, a Professor of Strategy and Director of Russian and Eurasian Studies at the US Army War College in Carlyle, Pennsylvania from 1996-2017, states: *Meaningful security guarantees for Ukraine can only be provided by NATO, but there will be serious political and operational constraints to any large-scale use of Alliance forces in the Eurasian steppe. Moscow has committed itself to a national military strategy that emphasizes reliance upon tactical nuclear weapons in a phase of conventional weakness. Assertive military commitments in areas immediately contiguous to the Russian border will therefore pose considerable risk. Moscow is willing and able to assert meaningful pressure in close proximity to its frontiers, and in the central European corridor it can be counted upon to do so if vital interests are perceived to be at stake. Zero-sum competition for Ukraine's heart and mind is therefore a dangerous game. "Washington's inclusion of the region near Russia's borders as vital US security interests or targets for expanding US influence," writes Sergo Mikoyan, "will make managing regional conflicts in these areas more difficult, if not impossible."*

In 2014, Russia accused the United States of supporting the overthrow of pro-Russian Ukrainian president Viktor Yanukovych, but the White House never officially declared that it no longer recognized Yanukovych as Ukraine's legitimate president. A US spokesperson would go as far as to state: "Mr. Yanukovych lost legitimacy as the leader of Ukraine," Shortly thereafter, however, Russia would annex Crimea and then instigate a civil war in eastern Ukraine.

In 2016, Donald Trump would become president of the United States, running on a platform to make America great again. Much of

President Trump's policy was an attempt to emulate the policy goals of former President Ronald Reagan, and shift away from the multilateralism that defined Obama's foreign policy. Trump aimed to do this by bringing the US back to the unilateral approach applied by previous republican presidents. Much like George W Bush, President Trump was uncomfortable with having to compromise US initiative for the sake of cooperating with international organizations. Trump also applied a strategy that gave less importance to diplomacy and more credence to defense. When he first got in office, he reversed the decision to withdraw US Troops from Syria and Iraq, and he also removed aid barriers levied upon Saudi Arabia and Bahrain. He took on a very conciliatory approach with Vladimir Putin and advocated a preference for leaders who could display a certain amount of savvy and strength, leaders such as Al-Sisi in Egypt, Duterte in the Philippines, and Erdogan in Turkey. Trump conveyed with conviction that his policies would be aimed to put America first when it came to foreign relations. Thus in 2018, his budget proposal cut spending on most government agencies, except the Department of Defense, the Department of Homeland Security, and the Department of Veteran Affairs. In late 2017, making a seemingly sudden u-turn on his pro-Putin perspective, Trump approved a plan to send lethal military aid to Ukraine, arms which included sniper rifles and Javelin anti-tank missiles, all aimed to help Ukraine fight against the Russia-backed separatists in the Donbas region. This move by the Trump administration increased US involvement in Ukraine's geopolitical affairs with Russia, and alarmed the Russian state who initially thought Trump was a supporter of Russian policy. The move also did not figure into the US media's narrative that Trump was pro-Russian. It became impossible to explain the juxtaposition of Trump's pro-Putin rhetoric and his anti-Russian policy. The tenure of Donald Trump and the early part of the Biden administration would prove to have devastating consequences for the security of eastern Europe. Trump, during his tenure, also harshly criticized NATO, considering it outdated. President Trump would often point out how the US is shouldering much of the military defense aspect of NATO policy, while other member nations like Germany are taking advantage by spending less on their own defense. This rhetoric would have major consequences and ultimately set Germany on the path to economic, military, and political independence.

In 2019, when Vlodymyr Zelensky became president of Ukraine, president Donald Trump became embroiled in a quid pro quo scandal which violated the US law that a sitting president is not to seek foreign help to win an election. After Biden declared his intention to run for president in 2020, Trump asked Zelensky via telephone that he investigate Joe Biden's involvement in the legal proceedings of an energy company in Ukraine that his son, Hunter Biden, worked at while Biden was Vice President during Obama's tenure. Trump then threatened to cut billions in military aid to Ukraine if Zelensky did not comply. This led to Trump getting impeached in 2020. He was later acquitted.

The global COVID-19 pandemic was the global spread of a deadly coronavirus strain which started in Wuhan, China. The virus began to spread to the rest of the world starting around January 15th of 2020. Throughout the time of the pandemic, NATO was still conducting aggressive military exercises near Russia's borders, and refused to agree to Russia's proposals for both nations to scale down military exercises. Meanwhile, in defiance of numerous US allies, President Trump pulled the US out of the 1992 Open Skies Treaty in late 2020. Mike Pompeo, US secretary of State from 2018-2021, asserted that Russia had not been in compliance due to the fact that they were imposing unilateral restrictions. The treaty was a confidence building instrument and allowed all 34 member states in the treaty to conduct joint observation flights over each other's territory and observe the activities of military personnel there. It was essentially a trust building exercise and meant to cultivate multilateralism. Any images compiled during the observational flights could be transmitted to any nation in the treaty. Both the US and Russia had placed some unilateral restriction on some areas of their respective territories. Furthermore, the US was eager to withdraw from the treaty so that they could stop spending resources on upgrading the observational aircraft, which they considered outdated. The House Foreign Affairs Committee Chairman Eliot Engel (D-N.Y.) and Rep. William Keating (D-Mass.) sharply criticized the move by the Trump administration, stating in statement issued on November 23, 2020 that "President Trump is attempting to burn down our critical institutions on his way out the door," they wrote. "In doing so, he not only jeopardized U.S. national security, but he blatantly ignored and deliberately broke the law." This occurred a year after the Trump Administration pulled out of another treaty with Russia, the 1987 INF Treaty. The INF treaty banned ground-launched intermediate range ballistic missiles. The US accused Russia in 2014 of violating the treaty by testing a cruise missile. Russia, on the other hand, accused the US of violating the treaty by setting up nuclear defense systems in eastern Europe. Many fear that without the treaty, there would be no limit as to how far nuclear weapons proliferation would go.

After vowing to keep US soldiers in Syria, President Trump decided in October of 2019 to withdraw the remaining US troops from Syria. In recent years up onto that point, the US had been launching airstrikes in Syria and also kept a number ground troops stationed there in the fight against ISIS. One of the US's closest partners during the campaign were the Kurdish fighters, thousands of whom have been killed in Syria since 2014. They were leading a coalition of multi-ethnic fighters called the Syrian Democratic Forces. In 2019, however, Turkey was preparing to launch an offensive in the region to repel the Kurdish presence near Turkey's border. The Kurdish militia serving alongside the US and leading the Syrian Democratic Forces in Syria was known as the YPG, a group that Turkey's president, Recep Erdogan, believes is simply an offshoot of the PKK, a group that both the US and Turkey has designated as a terrorist group. And the fact that the US was allied with the group during the Syrian campaign created a tension between the US and Turkey that became unsustainable. Thus Erdogan made it clear to Trump that Turkey was going to attack the Syrian border regardless of US presence. After a phone call with the Turkish president on this matter, Trump ordered the removal of the remaining 1000 US troops in Syria, and many US soldiers felt as though they were abandoning their closest ally and leaving them to be slaughtered by the Turkish army. The US would later confirm that the Kurdish fighters they cooperated with in Syria were an offshoot of the PKK, a US designated terrorist group. All things considered, the string of treaty violations and abandonment of partnership obligations conducted by the Trump administration, paved the way for the irreversible loss of trust between the United States and overseas partners. This loss of trust would reach a tipping point during the next administration to take office in Washington D.C.

When Joseph Biden became president of the US in 2020 and took office in 2021, he hesitated to reestablish similar multilateral treaties to the ones that the previous administration withdrew the US from. He also pursued a combative stance against other world leaders such as President Vladimir Putin of Russia and the Saudi Crown Prince Mohammad Bin Salman. In an interview in March of 2021, Biden referred to Putin as a "killer" and threatened to impose reprisals on him for interfering in the 2020 election. Shortly afterwards, 27 political organizations wrote to Biden urging him to scale down his combative rhetoric. In a statement issue by them in March of 2021, they stated: "*As national organizations that advocate for diplomacy, arms control, disarmament and peace, we are deeply alarmed by the recent negative exchanges between leaders of the two countries with more than 90 percent of the world's nuclear warheads in their arsenals,...."As Americans, we urge the Biden administration to stop participating in such reckless rhetorical exchanges and to instead vigorously pursue nuclear-arms negotiations with the Russian government,*" Some of groups involved included Justice Democrats, Blue America, Demand Progress, Our Revolution and Progressive Democrats of America. Alan Minsky, the executive director of the Progressive Democrats of

America said in the statement *"The grassroots progressive base of the Democratic Party has zero interest in a bellicose foreign policy towards Putin or Russia,......"What people want is a safer world with international cooperation, which will allow all of us to rebound more quickly from the public health and economic catastrophe of the past year. We have no patience for Cold War saber-rattling, let alone nuclear brinkmanship,"* Biden later clarified the "killer" remark during a phone conversation directly with Putin in June of 2021.

The US military pulled out of Afghanistan on August 30, 2021, ending a 20 year military operation there. After successfully overthrowing the Taliban in 2001, the remaining US military presence in the region could be defined by a long arduous process of trying to stabilize Afghanistan's new pro-democracy government. Throughout that time, the Taliban, though removed from power, remained a consistent threat to the newly installed government and was able to regain some lost territories. In February of 2020, the Trump administration and the Taliban confirmed an accordance known as the Doha Agreement, which established that the US would remove all of its troops from the Afghanistan region if the Taliban agrees to restrict Al Qaeda from operating in Taliban-held areas, as well as pursue ceasefire agreements with the new Afghan government. This correspondence between the Trump administration and the Taliban did not involve the Afghan government. Under the Doha agreement, the US would reduce US troop presence in Afghanistan from 13000 to 8600 by July 2020 and remove the remaining by May 1 2021. When Biden entered office, the number of US troops in Afghanistan had been reduced to 2500, but a month before the deadline established in the Doha agreement, Biden decided to extend the target date for withdrawal to September of 2021. On May 1st, however, which was the deadline for US troop withdrawal initially agreed upon by both Trump and the Taliban, the Taliban launched an offensive and in July, NATO would forecast that the Taliban would reclaim Afghanistan within weeks after full US withdrawal. However, the Taliban advance transpired much faster than anticipated. Consequently, the US attempted to facilitate the evacuation of embassy workers, US citizens, and Visa applicants as quickly as possible by deploying close to 5000 US troops to Kabul airport. 2000 more would be deployed following the Taliban's recapture of Kabul on August 15th. General Sami Sadat of the Afghan army considered US withdrawal as a betrayal of the Afghan army and stated to the New York Times that the agreement orchestrated by President Trump, as well as Biden's statement "American troops cannot and should not be fighting in a war and dying in a war that Afghan forces are not willing to fight for themselves." only emboldened the Taliban. He also mentioned that the 17000

personnel contractors that left Afghanistan in July, took with them critical weapons like helicopter missile defense and tracking technologies. Ashraf Ghani, president of Afghanistan prior to the Taliban takeover, would assert that the US's abrupt withdrawal gave momentum to the Taliban. Shortly after the Taliban takeover, a suicide bombing occurred at Hamid Karzai International Airport on August 26, 2021, killing 13 US military personnel and 70 Afghan citizens. The last plane to leave Kabul airport departed on August 30, 2021.

In retrospect, we can see how the abandonment of multilateral efforts in favor of a unilateral approach could exacerbate geopolitical tensions, and also undermine critical alliances, especially when the breach of contract is blatant. Both of these aspects—unilateral insistence and breach of treaty, along with a willingness to abandon allies abruptly—cultivate a sense a sense of fear and mistrust. This growing aspect in US foreign policy reached its most critical stage during the Biden Administration when after assuring Ukrainian President Zelensky that the US would act "swiftly and decisively" if Russia invades his country, Biden refused to intervene militarily when Russia did launch a full-scale invasion of Ukraine on February 24, 2022. Zelensky would state shortly thereafter "We have been left alone to defend our state," This failure of the US to once again uphold a promise had a negative residual effect on the sentiments of US allies. The most critical ally of the US, Saudi Arabia, in March of 2022 considered selling oil to the Chinese for Chinese Yuan instead of US dollars, a move that would topple the United States economy. The US failure on the Ukraine crisis will affect the international standing of the United States in the long run, and many nations will hesitate to establish any bilateral relations with them, which in the long term will eventually lead to the US becoming a pariah state. The US is now in danger of losing its economic and military super power status, while at the same time, being completely oblivious to the implications of Germany's effort to beef up their own military arsenal and reestablish themselves as a major military force in western Europe. This combined with the fact of Germany's economic leverage in western Europe as the top economy and one of the top creditor nations in the eurozone, leaves it all the more likely that Germany will eventually attempt to leave the eurozone or assume control of the European Central Bank, and also usurp the United States' position as Saudi Arabia's most important ally.

Chapter 11: The Rise of American Marxism

The case for a rising Marxist movement in America can be extrapolated from an excerpt of John Maynard Keynes's book "The Economic Consequences of the Peace." Here it lays out the groundwork for the rise and fall of a capitalist system:

Europe was so organized socially and economically as to secure the maximum accumulation of capital. While there was some continuous improvement in the daily conditions of life of the mass of the population, Society was so framed as to throw a great part of the increased income into the control of the class least likely to consume it. The new rich of the nineteenth century were not brought up to large expenditures, and preferred the power which investment gave them to the pleasures of immediate consumption. In fact, it was precisely the inequality of the distribution of wealth which made possible those vast accumulations of fixed wealth and of capital improvements which distinguished that age from all others. Herein lay, in fact, the main justification of the Capitalist System. If the rich had spent their new wealth on their own enjoyments, the world would long ago have found such a régime intolerable. But like bees they saved and accumulated, not less to the advantage of the whole community because they themselves held narrower ends in prospect.

The immense accumulations of fixed capital which, to the great benefit of mankind, were built up during the half century before the war, could never have come about in a Society where wealth was divided equitably. The railways of the world, which that age built as a monument to posterity, were, not less than the Pyramids of Egypt, the work of labor which was not free to consume in immediate enjoyment the full equivalent of its efforts.

Thus this remarkable system depended for its growth on a double bluff or deception. On the one hand the laboring classes accepted from ignorance or powerlessness, or were compelled, persuaded, or cajoled by custom, convention, authority, and the well-established order of Society into accepting, a situation in which they could call their own very little of the cake that they and Nature and the capitalists were co-operating to produce. And on the other hand the capitalist classes were allowed to call the best part of the cake theirs and were theoretically free to consume it, on the tacit underlying condition that they consumed very little of it in practice. The duty of "saving" became nine-tenths of virtue and the growth of the cake the object of true religion. There grew round the non-consumption of the cake all those instincts of puritanism which in other ages has withdrawn itself from the world and has neglected the arts of production as well as those of enjoyment. And

so the cake increased; but to what end was not clearly contemplated. Individuals would be exhorted not so much to abstain as to defer, and to cultivate the pleasures of security and anticipation. Saving was for old age or for your children; but this was only in theory,—the virtue of the cake was that it was never to be consumed, neither by you nor by your children after you.

In writing thus I do not necessarily disparage the practices of that generation. In the unconscious recesses of its being Society knew what it was about. The cake was really very small in proportion to the appetites of consumption, and no one, if it were shared all round, would be much the better off by the cutting of it. Society was working not for the small pleasures of to-day but for the future security and improvement of the race,—in fact for "progress." If only the cake were not cut but was allowed to grow in the geometrical proportion predicted by Malthus of population, but not less true of compound interest, perhaps a day might come when there would at last be enough to go round, and when posterity could enter into the enjoyment of our labors. In that day overwork, overcrowding, and underfeeding would have come to an end, and men, secure of the comforts and necessities of the body, could proceed to the nobler exercises of their faculties. One geometrical ratio might cancel another, and the nineteenth century was able to forget the fertility of the species in a contemplation of the dizzy virtues of compound interest.

There were two pitfalls in this prospect: lest, population still outstripping accumulation, our self-denials promote not happiness but numbers; and lest the cake be after all consumed, prematurely, in war, the consumer of all such hopes.

But these thoughts lead too far from my present purpose. I seek only to point out that the principle of accumulation based on inequality was a vital part of the pre-war order of Society and of progress as we then understood it, and to emphasize that this principle depended on unstable psychological conditions, which it may be impossible to recreate. It was not natural for a population, of whom so few enjoyed the comforts of life, to accumulate so hugely. The war has disclosed the possibility of consumption to all and the vanity of abstinence to many. Thus the bluff is discovered; the laboring classes may be no longer willing to forego so largely, and the capitalist classes, no longer confident of the future, may seek to enjoy more fully their liberties of consumption so long as they last, and thus precipitate the hour of their confiscation.

There is without question that the chain of crisis events over a short period of time in the United States will have a significant impact on how consumers approach their personal monetary behaviors. Events such as the fragmentation of the country along political and ethnic lines; the overwhelming number of mass

shootings in the country; violent riots and re-surging homicide rates; a global COVID-19 pandemic in which America would fare the worst, suffering the highest death rate among all countries; a war in eastern Europe at risk of igniting worldwide conflict of nuclear proportions. All of these will lead to what Keynes describes in "The Economic Consequences of the Peace." The sense of impending doom that will underscore in the minds of many the "vanity of abstinence", which will thus magnify the importance of consumption. And as those who wield the power of fixed capital become no longer "confident of the future", their choice "to enjoy more fully their liberties of consumption so long as they last" could ignite a sober awareness of wealth inequality that would precipitate what Karl Marx would define as the proletariat revolution. The revocation of the virtue status that once came with vigorous saving and abstinence, followed by the rise, from among the wealthier classes, of an ostentatious spending and consuming amid a growing loss of confidence in the future, is what will set the stage for class warfare and a very real communist revolution in the United States.

Chapter 12: A Second Coming of the Non-Aggression Pact

When it comes to a second non-aggression pact between Germany and Russia, we can look back at Keynes, and see that he was well aware of the importance of German/Russia relations on the world's economic climate. He writes in "The Economic Consequences of the Peace": *I see no possible means of repairing this loss of productivity within any reasonable period of time except through the agency of German enterprise and organization. It is impossible geographically and for many other reasons for Englishmen, Frenchmen, or Americans to undertake it;—we have neither the incentive nor the means for doing the work on a sufficient scale. Germany, on the other hand, has the experience, the incentive, and to a large extent the materials for furnishing the Russian peasant with the goods of which he has been starved for the past five years, for reorganizing the business of transport and collection, and so for bringing into the world's pool, for the common advantage, the supplies from which we are now so disastrously cut off. It is in our interest to hasten the day when German agents and organizers will be in a position to set in train in every Russian village the impulses of ordinary economic motive. This is a process quite independent of the governing authority in Russia; but we may surely predict with some certainty that, whether or not the form of communism represented by Soviet government proves permanently suited to the Russian temperament, the revival of trade, of the comforts of life and of ordinary economic motive are not likely to promote the extreme forms of those doctrines of violence and tyranny which are the children of war and of despair.*

Let us then in our Russian policy not only applaud and imitate the policy of non-intervention which the Government of Germany has announced, but, desisting from a blockade which is injurious to our own permanent interests, as well as illegal, let us encourage and assist Germany to take up again her place in Europe as a creator and organizer of wealth for her Eastern and Southern neighbors.

There are many persons in whom such proposals will raise strong prejudices. I ask them to follow out in thought the result of yielding to these prejudices. If we oppose in detail every means by which Germany or Russia can recover their material well-being, because we feel a national, racial, or political hatred for their populations or their Governments, we must be prepared to face the consequences of such feelings. Even if there is no moral solidarity between the nearly-related races of Europe, there is an economic solidarity which we cannot disregard. Even now, the world markets are one. If we do not allow Germany to exchange products with Russia and so feed herself, she must inevitably compete with us for the produce of the New World. The more successful we are in snapping economic relations between Germany and Russia, the more we shall depress the level of our own economic standards and increase the gravity of our own domestic problems. This is to put the issue on its lowest grounds. There are other arguments, which the most obtuse cannot ignore, against a policy of spreading and encouraging further the economic ruin of great countries.

These words by Keynes hold true in the world today, a world that is witnessing Russia exert aggression against its foremost western neighbor in Ukraine. The thesis of this book, one which foresees Germany competing directly with the US for mideast influence is right on line with Keynes when he says: *"If we do not allow Germany to exchange products with Russia and so feed herself, she must inevitably compete with us for the produce of the New World."* This statement in itself affirms the thesis that Germany will without question look to undercut US interests in the middle east and set up a petroeuro or petrodeutschmark deal with Saudi Arabia, replacing and phasing out the old petrodollar agreement.

As the US fades from international affairs, it becomes clear how the US is setting up its own economic and domestic demise. It becomes predictable that the Russian ruble will recover via Russia withholding fertilizer from the US and thus taking over the ethanol market by way of their wheat and corn surplus. This would coincide with Germany's military, political, and economic expansion in western Europe and Saudi Arabia selling oil for the German currency in exchange for security guarantees from Germany. Both Germany and Russia share the same goals of a multipolar, multilateral world, and could look to reestablish the non-aggression pact, along with an economic agreement and secret protocol outlining their respective spheres of influence. Central Africa will be the platform for this to happen, since the sustainment of a multipolar world will require deterring the one entity that insists on continuing its unipolar moment. The manner of which this would be achieved is by controlling the supply of one of the most critical minerals for military potency. That mineral is cobalt.

The new non-aggression pact involving Germany, Russia, and the Democratic Republic of Congo(DRC) could orchestrate a peace plan in which Russia would be allowed to mine cobalt in the Congo in exchange for Russia providing military support to the DRC and allowing the DRC president to mediate in Russian geopolitical crises. China would continue to develop infrastructure in the Congo, while Germany would provide to the DRC arms purchased from Ukraine, in exchange for being allowed to build a dam in the Congo to develop green hydrogen, with the option of purchasing cobalt directly from either Chinese or Russian mining companies operating in the Congo.

Under this deal, Ukraine's economy is bolstered by establishing

an arms export industry, of which Germany becomes its number one client through buying arms from Ukraine and shipping them to central Africa. This arrangement would be detailed in Germany's new non-aggression pact with Russia. Once the major portion of the Ukraine/Russia war settles down, Ukraine will have amassed a large scale military arsenal supplied to them by the United States and much of western Europe, setting the stage for Ukraine to become the top net exporter of arms.

The conflict in Ukraine, from the civil war in eastern Ukraine in 2014 up unto the Russian invasion of Ukraine in 2022 has underscored the need to bolster Ukraine's army and defense capabilities. Much of this necessity will eventually fall on the shoulders of Ukraine's military industrial complex through weapons production, modernization, and repair. But since the Russian invasion of the country in 2022, Ukraine's demand for arms has exceeded its supply, and due to this, they will become in the near future a net importer of arms, indicative of the fact that they still have to pay for the arms supplied to them by the west in response to the Russian invasion. The civil war in eastern Ukraine in 2014 and the Russian invasion of Ukraine in 2022 had led to a collapse of Ukraine's arms export market, falling from a previous position of being ranked in the top 10 of world leaders in arms exports. In 2012, before the civil war in Donbas, Ukraine was the world's fourth largest arms exporter. Furthermore, in order for Ukraine's army to become competitive in the global arms market, weapons manufacturers in the region will have to produce arms on par with the technological level of arms being imported. This will require a certain degree of reverse engineering. This realization of Ukraine's arms export potential now that its supply of weapons has increased exponentially becomes relevant, and the economics of recovery are still issues that have to be addressed. Ukraine has trailed the world's top technologically advanced nations in terms of arms production, and most of the weapons produced by Ukraine's military industrial complex were Soviet era with a few minor upgrades. But now with the war in Ukraine in 2022, Ukraine domestic arms manufacturers will have access to new technologies.

The US trying to lead the crusade in pushing for low to no cobalt cathode materials for EV batteries. The only promising prospect seems to be high nickel or high maganese cathode materials. Still and all, the US is not a major extractor of nickel and will likely remain relegated to foreign reliance on the material. The difference between nickel and cobalt in terms of US import is that it would be easier for the US to secure imports of nickel from Canada, than cobalt from central Africa. The other option is manganese. Batteries that contain a high manganese cathode is safer and cheaper than ones with high nickel cathode materials. However, when it comes to

battery research, there is always a trade-off. In this case of higher manganese, increasing the level of manganese decreases the cathode's stability, which will effect its performance. US defense is funding research into manganese cathodes for batteries in order to reduce their reliance on battery imports from China. Successful implementation of manganese, which is more widely available on earth than cobalt, would reduce an overall reliance on cobalt from the Congo. While many are confident in research concerning manganese use in EV batteries, there are still issues with stability that have not been resolved.

The Congo has 70% of the world's cobalt supply, which is the most critical element in lithium batteries, as it keeps them from overheating and catching fire. If Russia gains access to the cobalt reserves in the Congo, they will have some influence on China's lithium battery exports, and thus the defense capabilities of most countries because the vast majority of modern military equipment is reliant on battery powered electricity. At the moment, China has most of the influence in this regard as the top lithium battery and lithium hydroxide exporter. If the Congo offers to the Russians access to its cobalt reserves, Russia will have similar leverage against the west that China has, and this will most likely pressure more western nations to be just as careful with Russia as they are with China as to not upset the economic arrangement. These dependencies seem to be the only deterrent to major wars breaking out.

At the moment all the purported Cobalt substitutes have yet to match cobalt when it comes to battery life and cycle life, both of which are imperative for US defense systems, prolonged missions, and long distance EV. While domestic/home use of cobalt free batteries may be feasible in the near term, the lower energy density of cobalt free batteries will leave our most critical industries having to rely for some time on batteries that have adequate cobalt. If China and Russia gain control over much of the world's cobalt reserves, US national defense will be economically reliant on those countries for the upkeep of their own defense capabilities. In this case, China and Russia would have more leverage in deterring reckless US foreign policy.

Bibliography

all sources below used for paraphrasing and explaining topics in this book

https://www.sandstoneam.com/insight/rise-of-the-petrodollar
THE U.S. DOLLAR'S ROLE AS THE WORLD'S RESERVE CURRENCY WAS FIRST ESTABLISHED IN 1944 WITH THE BRETTON WOODS AGREEMENT(page 9 uses this source to explain 1973 petrodollar agreement)

Kevin L. Kliesen and David C. Wheelock, "Managing a New Policy Framework: Paul Volcker, the St. Louis Fed, and the 1979-82 War on Inflation," Federal Reserve Bank of St. Louis Review, First Quarter 2021, pp. 71-97. https://doi.org/10.20955/r.103.71-97 (pages 9-10 uses this source to explain Volcker and interest rates)

Wikipedia contributors. (2021, September 10). 1973–1974 stock market crash. In Wikipedia, The Free Encyclopedia. Retrieved 21:19, March 10, 2022, from https://en.wikipedia.org/w/index.php?title=1973%E2%80%931974_stock_market_crash&oldid=1043567392

Wikipedia contributors. (2022, March 8). Gulf War. In Wikipedia, The Free Encyclopedia. Retrieved 21:20, March 10, 2022, from https://en.wikipedia.org/w/index.php title=Gulf_War&oldid=1075986328 (page 11 uses this source to explain gulf war)

“The Mars Hypothesis” by Anthony of Boston (Much of Chapter 1 copies directly from this source with permission from the author)

“What sanctions are being imposed on Russia over Ukraine invasion?” https://www.bbc.com/news/world-europe-60125659 (pg 22 uses this source to explain sanctions against Russia)

“Reduce the Pentagon’s Dependence on China by Recharging US Battery, Electronics Industry” by Jeffrey Nadaner https://www.defenseone.com/ideas/2021/07/reduce-pentagons-dependence-china-recharging-us-battery-electronics-industry/183729/ (pages 25 and 26 uses this source to explain battery importance on US defense)

“Before invasion, Ukraine’s lithium wealth was drawing global attention” Written by Hiroko Tabuchi https://indianexpress.com/article/world/before-invasion-ukraines- lithium-wealth-was-drawing-global-attention-

7799024/ (page 26 uses this for stating 500,000 tons lithium oxide in eastern Ukraine)

"Chinese Company Removed as Operator of Cobalt Mine in Congo" New York Times article by
By Eric Lipton and Dionne Searcey
https://www.nytimes.com/2022/02/28/world/congo-cobalt-mining- china.html (page 26 -27 uses this to explain China cobalt mine)

Bernstein, Edward. "Reflections on Bretton Woods." In The International Monetary System: Forty Years After Bretton Woods, 15-20. Boston: Federal Reserve Bank of Boston, May 1984. (page 8 uses this source)

Bordo, Michael D. "Gold Standard." In The Concise Encyclopedia of Economics. Library of Economics and Liberty. Article published 2008.

Bordo, Michael, Owen Humpage, and Anna J. Schwartz, "U.S. Intervention during the Bretton Wood Era: 1962-1973," Working Paper 11-08, Federal Reserve Bank of Cleveland, Cleveland, Ohio, April 2011.

ARGONNE NATIONAL LABORATORY
Researchers eye manganese as key to safer, cheaper lithium-ion batteries BY CHRISTINA NUNEZ|JUNE 4, 2020
https://www.anl.gov/article/researchers-eye-manganese-as-key-to-safer-cheaper-lithiumion-batteries

Eichengreen, Barry. Exorbitant Privilege: The Rise and Fall of the Dollar and the Future of the International Monetary System. New York: Oxford University Press, 2011.

"Oil, weapons and realpolitik: Why some countries want to stay on friendly terms with Russia" By Dan De Luce
https://www.nbcnews.com/news/world/even-us-allies-are-reluctant-confront-russia-invasion-ukraine-rcna20686

Lessons from the Collapse of the Ruble Zone
Anders Aslund PDF https://www.ifo.de/DocDL/forum-2016-4-aslund-ruble-zone-collapse-december.pdf

Afghan commander says army was 'betrayed by politics and

presidents' BY MYCHAEL SCHNELL - 08/25/21 2:10 PM ET https://thehill.com/policy/international/569386-afghan-commander-says-army-was-betrayed-by-politics-and-presidents/

Wikipedia contributors. (2022, March 21). Withdrawal of United States troops from Afghanistan (2020–2021). In Wikipedia, The Free Encyclopedia. Retrieved 15:04, April 9, 2022, from https://en.wikipedia.org/w/index.php?title=Withdrawal_of_United_States_troops_from_Afghanistan_(2020%E2%80%932021)&oldid=1078361536

Twin Deficits and the Fate of the US Dollar: A Hard Landing Reexamined by Rod Thompson
https://jpia.princeton.edu/sites/jpia/files/2008-6.pdf

https://www.forbes.com/sites/afontevecchia/2011/09/08/what-would-happen-if-germany-seceded-from-the-eu/

https://www.dw.com/en/germany-commits-100-billion-to-defense-spending/a-60933724

Kenen, Peter. "Bretton Woods System." In The New Palgrave Dictionary of Economics, Second Edition, edited by Steven N. Durlauf and Lawrence E. Blume. Palgrave Macmillan, 2008.

Meltzer, Allan H. "U.S. Policy in the Bretton Woods Era." Federal Reserve Bank of St. Louis Review 73, no. 3 (May/June 1991): 54-83.

Patinkin, Don. "Keynes, John Maynard (1883–1946)." In The New Palgrave Dictionary of Economics, Second Edition, edited by Steven N. Durlauf and Lawrence E. Blume. Palgrave Macmillan, 2008.

Stasi State or Workers' Paradise – socialism in the German Democratic Republic and what became of it
by Bruni de la Motte & John Green
First published in Britain in 2015
Copyright © John Green & Bruni de la Motte

Wikipedia contributors. (2021, July 21). Economic history of the German reunification. In Wikipedia, The Free Encyclopedia. Retrieved 13:49, April 4, 2022, from
https://en.wikipedia.org/w/index.php?

title=Economic_history_of_the_German_reunification&oldid=1034725466

April 2019 Country report Middle East and North Africa Department "Saudi Arabia's Perspectives on Germany: Perceptions and Future Potential for Cooperation" written by René Rieger & Sebastian Sons(pages 14-18 uses this source to explain Germany's relations with Saudi Arabia)

Caldwell, P. C., & Hanshew, K. (2018). Germany since 1945: Politics, culture, and society. (pages 58 and 59 uses this book to explain west german constitution)

"World's largest hydro dam 'could send cheap green hydrogen from Congo to Germany'" By Bernd Radowitz https://www.rechargenews.com/transition/worlds-largest-hydro-dam- could-send-cheap-green-hydrogen-from-congo-to-germany/2-1-871059

Creation of the Bretton Woods System by Sandra Kollen Ghizoni, Federal Reserve Bank of Atlanta https://www.federalreservehistory.org/essays/bretton-woods-created (pages 7 – 9 in Chapter 1 uses this source)

Ousted President Is 'Ready To Fight For The Future Of Ukraine' February 28, 20148:30 AM ET MARK MEMMOTT https://www.npr.org/sections/thetwo-way/2014/02/28/283878194 /ousted-president-is-ready-to-fight-for-the-future-of-ukraine

US officials say lethal weapons headed to Ukraine https://www.cnbc.com/2017/12/23/us-officials-say-lethal-weapons-headed-to-ukraine.html

Fedir Zhuravka, Rostislav Botvinov, Marharyta Parshyna, Tetiana Makarenko and Natalia Nebaba (2021). Ukraine's integration into the world arms market. Innovative Marketing , 17(4), 146-158. doi:10.21511/im.17(4).2021.13

https://www.bbc.com/news/world-15572775 Russia angry at Viktor Bout's US guilty verdict

June 2018 edition of the Finance and Development Journal pg 14

https://www.imf.org/external/pubs/ft/fandd/2018/06/pdf/fd0618.pdf

"Understanding Russian Priorities in Latin America" by Vladimir Rouvinski https://www.wilsoncenter.org/sites/default/files/media/documents/publication/ki_170117_cable_russia_latin_american_v1.pdf

(Document by R. Craig Nation is from NATO's official website nato.int) https://www.nato.int/cps/en/natohq/news_25864.htm?selectedLocale=en

Here is the url for the PDF: https://www.nato.int/acad/fellow/98-00/nation.pdf (pg 103 uses this source for quote about NATO provocation)

Wikipedia contributors. (2022, March 15). Houthi takeover in Yemen. In Wikipedia, The Free Encyclopedia. Retrieved 12:20, April 12, 2022, from https://en.wikipedia.org/w/index.php?title=Houthi_takeover_in_Yemen&oldid=1077329319 (pages 18 – 20 uses this source for information about Yemen)

Index

www.ingramcontent.com/pod-product-compliance
Lightning Source LLC
LaVergne TN
LVHW090103250926
848814LV00044B/3
* 9 7 9 8 3 3 0 5 1 7 4 9 7 *